ONE FLESH

ONE FLESH

Peter Sammons

Glory to Glory Publications

*Published in Great Britain by
Glory to Glory Publications, an imprint of Buy Research Ltd.*
**Glory to Glory Publications
PO Box 212 SAFFRON WALDEN CB10 2UU**

Publisher's Note

As with all Glory to Glory publications, throughout this
book the reader is asked to compare what is written with the
Bible, and if at any point a conflict is found to accept what is
written in Scripture.

ISBN 978-0-9567831-8-9

Printed in Great Britain by Imprint Digital, Exeter

Contents

*To Joyce, my lovely wife, without whom
this book would not have happened!*

FOREWORD

This short book is written in a lively, accessible and personal style. With a soupçon of personal experience, mixed in with a solid framework of biblical common-sense, Peter Sammons demonstrates that the whole issue of "one flesh" in a marriage relationship is simply nothing more – and nothing less – than God wanting the very best for us, rather than stifling us with the "dos" and "don'ts" that are the popular, and it must be said, mistaken, perception of Christian marriage.

This book really is suitable for all, whether or not the reader has made a commitment to marriage or has any sense of a personal relationship with Jesus Christ. It is a careful mix of biblical insight and practical advice. Sammons makes no claims to be any sort of an "agony uncle", but does answer many of the big questions that the vast majority of us will face at some time in our lives.

Peter Sammons demonstrates the relevance of biblical teaching to the problems and challenges faced by those of us struggling with relationships in the twenty-first century, as well as those at the threshold of relationship-building.

I wholeheartedly recommend this book, not just for those considering "taking the plunge", or even those who have already done so, but also for anyone interested in getting a clear sense of God's plan for nurturing and protecting relationships. For this is what Sammons demonstrates to be the will of God the Creator.

Steve Maltz

Author: *Jesus, Man of Many Names* (2007) and
God's Signature (2012)

INTRODUCTION

Living Happily Ever After

"And they all lived happily ever after – THE END".

These cosy words often finish a children's story. By implication living together happily ever after is the fictional 'outlook' for the hero and heroine at the end of just about every Hollywood and Bollywood romantic movie. But living happily seems in real life to be an elusive outcome. No one enters a relationship for it to go wrong; no one gets married in order to live miserably. There are many happy relationships, and many wonderful marriages. Yet there are just as many marriages that go wrong, if the statistics are to be believed.

This book is called "One Flesh". Christians believe that God created this world and that He created men and women, male and female, in His own image. He did not create us for miserable relationships – yet that is so often what we seem to end up with. He created us for good, useful and happy relationships. Most of all He created us for relationship with Himself.

So why is this book called "One Flesh"? Simply because that is what Jesus said that a male and female will become when the two are joined together. When he said that, he was quoting from the scriptures (actually from Genesis 2: 24) and by so doing he was agreeing with those scriptures and the reality expressed by the phrase. Believing, as Christians do, that God made us for good and happy lives, this book sets out to see what the Bible has to say about relationships, about love, about romance, about marriage. To do that we are going to explore what the Bible says in both the New and Old Testaments.

At the end of this book readers should at least get a sense of what the Bible actually says on these important questions. It is the hope and prayer of the author that readers will also get a clearer idea of how God wants them to live out their lives as regards the opposite sex. We will see some pitfalls to avoid and discover some principles which, if adopted, will help us to make good and healthy choices for the way we live our lives and with whom we share them.

At this point we may already have hit upon a problem: the reader may not believe in God! If that is your present position then you have two options – put down the book now and find another way to spend your next few evenings, or read on in the hope that you will get at least two worthwhile benefits: (1) You will better understand the attitude of Jesus to relationships; and (2) You may pick up some clues as to how to maximise your chances of living your life "happily ever after".

The author recognises that most readers will approach this book with limited knowledge of the Bible – and some will have absolutely no knowledge of it. These readers can have confidence that in working through this book they will pick up a little 'head knowledge' along the way. This is not going to be a crash course on the Bible or theology, but inevitably readers will gain some understanding of the Bible as they follow the argument. In this Introduction we will, however, make three simple observations about the Bible, so readers can get a clear sense of how the author approaches the subject.

The Bible is divided into Old and New Testaments

This immediately sounds rather obscure and the author acknowledges that these titles and divisions are not altogether helpful. The Old Testament tells of the dealings of God with humans in history, and especially through His chosen people – the Hebrews. The New Testament tells of God's dealings with mankind through Jesus, His Son, whom His followers called "Lord", as they acknowledged Him to be the ultimate authority over their lives. *Part* of the significance of the relationship between the "Old" and "New" Testaments could be expressed in these terms: "The Promise" (for the "Old") and "The Promise Fulfilled" (for the "New"). There is, of course, much more to both Testaments than that particular dimension of promise and fulfilment: we must always remember that the New Testament declaration that "all Scripture is God-breathed" is actually referring to what we call the "Old" Testament; and we learn a huge amount about God's nature and purposes from the "Old" as well as the "New". The *particular* Old Testament promise that I have in mind is that God would one day send a Saviour to the world, whilst the New reveals who that Saviour is. Admittedly, the expressions "Promise" and "Promise Fulfilled" are not altogether helpful, as some of the promises of the Old Testament (and indeed some promises in the New Testament) are yet to be fulfilled in the future. But you might find it useful to bear in mind those ideas of *promise* and *promise fulfilled* as you work through this book. It is one context in which to think about the sixty-six books that make up the Bible, and one way in which the two "Testaments" stand in relation to each other. They are interconnected in very many ways – the New does not replace the Old, it confirms it. *Hand in glove* might be a better analogy for the way the two "Testaments" relate to each other.

Just how do we read the Bible – and is it dependable anyway?

Let's just consider its dependability for a moment: in this book we do not set out to defend the Holy Scriptures as the definitive word of God. There are many good books that examine the Holy Bible in that context and no doubt someone who is genuinely interested in this subject will readily find what they need without having to look too hard. If the reader comes to this book with the objection that the Bible *is not*, or *may not be*, the sole revelation of "god" then he or she is invited simply to "park" that objection for the time being. There surely can be no great problem in looking closely at what the Scriptures have to say about love, romance and relationships so as to acquire a clear understanding of the argument being put forward in this book.

In a court of law as each witness gives their testimony a judge and jury will form an opinion as to the trustworthiness of that particular person, and the validity of the testimony they offer. The author invites the reader to adopt the same attitude towards the Bible. Readers can always "call more witnesses" at a later stage if they feel that the witness of Scripture is incomplete or invalid.

The key suggestion made by this author is that (for the purpose of this study) a doubter 'set aside' his or her doubts at this point, and for now proceed on the basic working assumption that the Scriptures are valid and trustworthy. In this way we use the Scriptures as the platform from which to review what God says to us about this question of "one flesh".

Allowing that many readers will be Westerners, some may feel that reference to God as 'Him' and 'He' represents some form of gender aggression. If so, you are simply invited to park that objection for the time being. We use those terms because the Bible does so. You can always reconsider your objection later if you feel that the gender question remains a challenge for you personally.

So how do we read the Bible?

In essence the way most serious Christians read the Bible is to take the text at its plainest and simplest meaning – in other words the way the writer clearly meant the words to be read and understood. We should only read the text in another way if it is quite obvious that the writer or the context demands that it be read differently. That is the approach adopted in this book.

Toulouse or To Lose – The A340-600 Toulouse incident

This might sound a very strange place to begin a book about relationships and romance, but hopefully it illustrates a point neatly. We are at the Airbus Technical Centre in Toulouse, France, on 15 November 2007. A brand new Airbus A340 is undergoing customer acceptance tests. The plane has never carried a passenger nor earned any revenue. It costs several hundreds of millions of dollars. The customer's flight crew and Airbus engineers are running through hundreds of tests. The engines are running at full throttle and the brakes are on. Suddenly the plane lurches forwards and runs headlong into a concrete barrier. The entire front of the plane is smashed up. Mercifully there are no fatalities although there are injuries. The plane is a write-off for insurance purposes.

Why did the accident happen? Who was to blame? It seems that in one way or another the relevant maker's instructions with regard to acceptance test procedures either were not read or, having been read, were not understood. So what has the Tolouse A340 incident got to do with love, romance and the idea of "one flesh"?

Only this: Christians believe that God, the Creator (or God the Maker) has given us His *maker's instructions*. If we ignore them we do so at our peril. Like the airliner we might end up trashing our relationships, our marriage and even our lives. If the Maker has given instructions, isn't it wise and prudent to make an effort to understand them? That's what we set out to do in this book, using the Bible as our guide.

There may perhaps be no greater tragedy than to build a relationship that is almost certain to fail, or to lose a relationship on which so many hopes have been founded, when we have an Eternal Father who wants His children to make the very best of their time in this world. He has given us wise counsel in His word – the Bible – and this guidance is not too difficult or too impenetrable for us to take note of it and seek to live by it. Do we use this guidance, or do we lose it in the headlong rush to seek and find "love"?

Most people will have at least a passing interest in this subject, whatever their age. And as most of us expect to enter into relationships, some of which may prove to be frivolous, others very serious; some sought out, and others thrust upon us, so very many people have some need and desire to understand this idea of two becoming "one flesh" and what that means in practice. A working assumption is that many readers will be young, but the principles explored are timeless and ageless. A second working assumption is general unfamiliarity with the Holy Bible, so we will work at a reasonably slow pace on this, giving those who know nothing of the Bible the chance to do some catching up.

If you are a young man and are facing a difficult choice as you consider the possibilities of striking up a relationship with Carol or Candida, Caroline or Cassandra, Celia or Chantelle, Chloe or Clarissa, will this book sort out the question for you? If you are a young lady and are considering the rival merits of Morgan or Michael, Murray or Melvin, Miles or Montague, Mungo or Murdoch, will this book sort out your problem (or opportunity?) It is unlikely if you are facing that sort of choice that a name will leap out from the pages of this book! But biblical principles as revealed in *the Maker's Instructions* will become apparent to you. Sometimes the likely reasons behind the Maker's Instructions will also suggest themselves to you. The joyous prospects of a *one flesh* relationship will hopefully become clearer to you. The dangers and possible sorrows of a wasted relationship will also become clearer, and hopefully will be more readily recognised as a snare to be avoided.

What of those who are single and happy to remain that way? Are they in some way "missing out" or are there joys in singleness that should not be overlooked? Once again it is hoped that this short book will set out good principles that can help those who are single, and wondering whether to remain so. So to all those, young and older, single or married, or courting, at the end of a relationship or at the beginning, you can rest assured that the God who is described in so many magnificent ways in the Bible, but perhaps most profoundly as a righteous God *who is love*, is a God Who wants something good and special just for you. If you look ultimately to Him, He will help you to build relationships that are worthwhile, happy, profitable – and indeed permanent, if that is your desire.

I had intended, in planning this book, to explore in some detail the Hebrew wedding rites as they were in the first century, to get a clearer sense of some of the things that Jesus taught about marriage and how relationships were formed in those days. However, this book is already long enough and sometimes, as they say, "less is more!" As this book was being prepared I had the great privilege of reading a draft of Stephanie Cottam's excellent short book *Ready or Not – He is Coming* and that settled the matter! Stephanie's book looks at Jesus' teaching that He, as Bridegroom, will one day return for His Bride, the church. Stephanie explores first century Hebrew marriage rites in splendid detail, drawing out many insights and lessons that would be obscure without some understanding of marriage as Jesus knew it. Rather than reinvent the proverbial wheel, I encourage readers to seek our *Ready or Not – He is Coming* for it is an excellent and really helpful book, at a number of different levels.

Pie in the Sky?

Can we really hope to live "happily ever after"? Should we dare to hope for such a thing or will we inevitably be disappointed and ultimately hurt? The author is a happily married man and whilst he might want to be thought of as the perfect partner and husband, reality suggests otherwise! As one vicar once said in commenting on marriage: "Where two sinners live in close proximity, the sparks are bound to fly!" Where there are humans in relation to each other there are likely to be problems, no matter how good they may be as individuals – and even where they are committed Christians. The author's own parents had what would in polite company be referred to as a "difficult marriage" – so it is not with an unrealistic or *pie in the sky* or other-worldly attitude that the author approaches this subject. Far from it. But he puts faith in the words of Jesus found in Matthew 11: 28–30: "**Come to me, all you who are weary and burdened, and I will give you rest. Take my yoke upon you and learn from me, for I am gentle and humble in heart, and you will find rest for your souls. For my yoke is easy and my burden is light.**" (NIV). That is what we can trust Jesus to do for us as we approach this vital subject of two becoming *one flesh*. As we consider it, as we work towards it, we can trust the Lord of Life is on our side and wants nothing but the best for us.

Ashdon, England 2012

"Happy are those who have been invited to the wedding feast"

1

ONE FLESH

Way back in the 1980s I began what has sometimes threatened to become a compulsive habit, namely collecting articles from newspapers and magazines and filing them away because they are "interesting" and may one day be useful. Whilst I have managed to keep my habit in the realms of reasonable behaviour (well, I haven't actually asked my wife but she does not complain too much), I now have several lever-arch files scattered around my home containing miscellaneous and quite random articles. As a friend once said, "When they carry you out 'feet forwards', that lot is likely to go straight in a waste bin!" Today I ensure that all these collected articles are inscribed with date and publication, so at least I know where they came from, and who I might need to thank or acknowledge if ever I use them as source material in a book.

I have one article, however, that regrettably I omitted to inscribe with date and publication, but which I have always found most intriguing. I cut the article from a UK newspaper in the early 1980s but have no idea which one it was. As I am going to quote it fully, I will apologise in advance to whichever newspaper it was from which I took that article, and the lack of proper "credit" for its source and date. The article itself gives no writer name, so presumably it was by a 'staff writer' – often known in the trade affectionately, or dismissively, as a 'newspaper hack'! It has this intriguing title: "**Husband saves his wife's life with the power of love**." In quoting from the article I have amended the names of the people involved and "censored" the name of the hospital, as I would not wish the individuals or their families to be in any way embarrassed by reference to their personal circumstances in this book, many years after the event.

As you read the article, have in your mind the phrase "one flesh".

Husband saves his wife's life with the power of love

A man has donated a kidney to save his wife's life – despite having the wrong tissue type.

Specialists believe that Helen ****, whose life was threatened when the search for a suitable donor became hopeless, was only able to accept her husband's kidney because the couple had been making love for more than 20 years.

Tissue profile is the most important predictor of the success or failure of a transplant operation. But renal specialist Dr Paul **** had seen "living transplants" between incompatible couples in America and was amazed by the results.

He believes that couples sharing bodily fluids build up a tolerance to each other, making the grafting more *successful. Mrs ****, 42, is already seeing the benefits of the pioneering operation and has been taken off dialysis.*

Today she said "I feel great now and I've got a lot more energy. We are both living fairly normal lives again".

She contracted a kidney disease when she fell pregnant with her son, George, now 10. Her kidneys failed completely seven years ago.

The procedure has become commonplace in the US and Japan, but only 12 operations of this kind were carried out in Britain last year.

*The couple, from ******, underwent surgery nine weeks ago and Mrs ****'s progress so far is "startling".*

Husbands and wives, living together for a long period, can grow more and more alike. It is a well observed phenomenon. Many people have commented before on how the two become more similar as they go through life – in tastes, sense of humour, social and political outlook. They can even begin to look the same! But the newspaper article above suggests that this 'oneness' can actually go much deeper than that. Their two bodies can become so attuned that they recognise each other as 'one', and physically at the 'tissue' level they become indistinguishable from each other. It is the Bible that speaks of men and women becoming "one flesh" – and this will be a recurrent theme throughout this book, although the full implication of this idea goes far beyond the purely physical. Could it really be that the writer of Genesis, some 4,000 years ago, was given a deeper insight into the nature of the male and female relationship that we 'modern' people are only just beginning to understand?

We will turn our attention now to considering the Bible's most foundational statement about those men and women who commit to each other as lifetime mates.

Starting at the beginning

Where do we learn most about the relationship of man to woman and woman to man – and of God's eternally designed intentions for them? The book of Genesis is the first book in the Bible – the first in the Old Testament. It is the first book of "the promise", if you prefer. Having pointed out in the introduction to this book that some readers may have real issues and problems if they do not actually believe in God, we immediately hit a fresh problem in this first chapter: we are going to look at the Bible's account of Creation and some readers may have fresh difficulty with this. Let us start with a thought about the book of Genesis: some Christians consider the book to be literally true and true in a 'linear sense'. In other words, the events described happened in the way described and in the order described. They take Genesis at its plainest possible reading. Others consider that the book reveals "truths" that are plain to see but not necessarily meant to be understood in a linear way – in other words the things described actually happened but not necessarily in a physical sense nor necessarily in a linear time-ordered sense.

Whichever way a reader chooses to look at Genesis, it does not make a big difference to the arguments set out in this book. There is a third way of reading and understanding Genesis, which is that both positions are true at the same time! Now this completely surprising thought takes some prayerful effort to really enter into. We only consider it here as there is a case for saying that sometimes positions that appear to be mutually exclusive are *not in fact* mutually exclusive. Some call such an approach a "Hebraic" mindset which is opposed to and in contrast to the Western "Greek" mindset, the latter totally dominating our modern world. Incidentally, the author is *not* suggesting that a Hebraic mindset *would* find that both the literal and metaphorical interpretations of Genesis are equally true. This is only suggested as it helps us to bypass an immediate and substantial 'problem' for some people – that of 'Creation' versus some other way of explaining our existence here on planet earth.

The author's view on Creation, for what it is worth, is not crucial to how this book develops its key themes. But he wants his readers to mark this. What Genesis tells us, emphatically, is that:

God created the world (*how* is not relevant to this book);
God created it with a good purpose;
God created it perfectly – such troubles as we recognise in the world result from mankind's resistance to God;
God created men and women for each other.

Very soon we will explore this aspect of being created *for* each other. But first one further word of explanation: throughout this book the author has chosen to use the *Good News* translation of the Bible – a translation which emerged over the period 1966 to 1971. Many will argue, and the author agrees 100% with them, that the *Good News* is a paraphrase rather than a translation. The reason why we use the *Good News* throughout this book is because this version is so easy to understand. In the context of our exploration of what the Lord Jesus taught about love, marriage, relationships and how men and women are meant (by God) to coexist and to prosper, there is no special teaching that depends on a particular translation, or a particular Greek or Hebrew word. In other words, precision in translating is not a key to understanding the full force of what Jesus taught on those matters.

So what does the Bible say? Where would you expect to find the answer? We go to the beginning of the Bible:

Genesis 1: 24–31(a)

Then God commanded, "Let the earth produce all kinds of animal life: domestic and wild, large and small" – and it was done. So God made them all, and he was pleased with what he saw. Then God said, "And now we will make human beings; they will be like us and resemble us. They will have power over the fish, the birds, and all animals, domestic and wild, large and small." So God created human beings, making them to be like himself. He created them male and female, blessed them, and said, "Have many children, so that your descendants will live all over the earth and bring it under their control. I am putting you in charge of the fish, the birds, and all the wild animals. I have provided all kinds of grain and all kinds of fruit for you to eat; but for all the wild animals and for all the birds I have provided grass and leafy plants for

food" – and it was done. God looked at everything he had made, and he was very pleased.

Diligent readers may want to go back and look at all of Genesis chapters 1 and 2 to get a clear insight into the whole sweep of the Creation event. But we start our review at verse 26 of Genesis 1. There seems to be a shift of gear between verse 25 and verse 26 – it is almost as though God has now reached the purpose of the whole creation exercise, and that purpose is: you and me! In Genesis chapter 2 we meet 'Adam' who is created specially and separately by God, created in God's own image. How the creation of Adam in chapter 2 relates to chapter 1 and verse 27 is obscure, so we waste no time in exploring that question. The key point in our reading above is that in Adam we meet not only a *homo sapiens* but also *homo spiritualis* – a man designed to know God in a personal way, a man with a spiritual dimension. Now we come to the key bit for our book. Readers may want to read this twice just to get the full flavour:

Genesis 2: 18–24
Then the Lord God said, "It is not good for the man to live alone. I will make a suitable companion to help him." So he took some soil from the ground and formed all the animals and all the birds. Then he brought them to the man to see what he would name them; and that is how they all got their names. So the man named all the birds and all the animals; but not one of them was a suitable companion to help him.

Then the Lord God made the man fall into a deep sleep, and while he was sleeping, he took out one of the man's ribs and closed up the flesh. He formed a woman out of the rib and brought her to him. Then the man said, "At last, here is one of my own kind – Bone taken from my bone, and flesh from my flesh. "Woman' is her name because she was taken out of man." That is why a man leaves his father and mother and is united with his wife, and they become one.

Having stated a few paragraphs above that the looser, paraphrased *Good News* version of the Bible is good enough to illustrate all that Jesus taught about relationships between men and women, I must now backtrack a little – in fact all of the main English language translations of the Bible render verse 24 as the man and woman becoming "one flesh". The *Good News* says "they became one". Both phrases say the same thing. But having chosen to call this book "One Flesh" it is vital that readers know where that phrase has come from, and that, as we use the phrase throughout this book, we also recognise that in a very real sense it means that a man and a woman merge into one in a way that transcends the purely physical.

So what does Genesis chapter 2 tell us about God's grand design for men and women? First and foremost is that man and woman were created to defeat loneliness. Let's dig into this a little deeper: the first thing we notice as we read about the creation of humans is that the names we so often recognise (Adam and Eve) are hardly mentioned in the Bible. The man is referred to simply as "the man" in most English translations. The name "Adam" is first encountered in *The New International Version* (for example) in Genesis 3: 20, but this is purely the choice of the translators. Scholars point out that the name "Adam" as a personal name is not encountered in the original Hebrew until Genesis 4: 25, whereas the Hebrew word for man (adam) sounds like and may be related to the Hebrew for ground (adamah). The word Adam in Hebrew is best translated "mankind", so the individual person Adam was and is still a real representative of all humans. It was God who named the man "Adam". Dear reader, we are not here trying to sort out all the theological and historical questions around Adam! We are only looking at Adam as being the most foundational way of understanding God's purposes for men and women. Adam was a real individual – and Jesus clearly saw him in that way. As we shall discover later, Jesus justified His view on marriage by speaking of the first couple, an allusion that would be meaningless if "Adam" were to have been just a myth or a spiritual symbol of some type.

Whilst God gave Adam his name, it was Adam who named Eve. Having been introduced to and given names to many animals, it is with a real excitement that Adam meets and is bowled-over by Eve, his special companion (Genesis 2: 23). It is only after Adam and Eve's rebellion against God, set out in Genesis chapter 3, and after God has pronounced judgement against the man and woman (and, we might add, against the serpent – the devil) that Adam finally gives his wife a name, just before they are banished forever from the Garden that God had given them. The Hebrew word "Eve" sounds similar to the Hebrew word "living", and Adam named her Eve because she was the "mother" of all the living – in other words the mother of all of mankind.

We have spent a few minutes looking at the background to this idea of one flesh, of *men and women being meant for each other*. I repeat that we are not trying to iron out all the questions that the biblical Creation account raises – there is certainly much more that could be said. But let us hold on for just a little longer as we conclude our introduction to Adam and Eve. Surprising as it may seem, the account we have in the Bible of Adam and Eve teaches us a great deal about how men and women are meant to relate to each other. The sole purpose of this book "One Flesh" is to help boys and girls, men and women to see that there are biblical principles that *we* can apply *today* in the search for a mate, and those principles are as relevant today as the day they were written. So what does the account of Adam and Eve in Genesis chapters 1– 3 tell us that we may be missing today?

The pattern established....

This is where the rubber really hits the road! The world at large has certain preconceived notions about courtship, relationship-forming and marriage. It goes something like this (and this is almost irrespective of culture): you are better off if your mate is young, healthy, attractive, brainy, wealthy. If you can find such a mate you stand the best possible "chance" of forming a happy, meaningful, fulfilling and lasting relationship. That is the world's view. But is it the Bible's view? And is it God's view?

We note in Genesis 2: 22 that God "**formed a woman out of the rib and brought her to him**". We note straight away that it is God who brings the woman to the man – Adam does not have to rush out and look for her. Perhaps, one might think, because Adam and Eve had brains, and in the absence of anyone similar, they would rapidly have reached the conclusion they were meant for each other. But it was God who did the bringing together. There is a key lesson here, at the very beginning of the Bible and the very first reference to men and women forming relationships, namely that God is sufficiently interested, sufficiently engaged, to do the bringing together. One question that Christians must ask themselves, but maybe non-Christian readers will also identify with this, is "Does God have "the right" mate for me?" And by this we mean the *specific* person God has chosen so as to bring out the best opportunity for me to form a brilliant relationship that will lead to happiness and will stand the test of time. I will venture that the answer is no! And for this reason – you are asking the right question, but in the wrong way.

For a start you are asking with a selfish motive – what is going to work for *me*? Your question is egocentric. If you go into a relationship with the sole aim of bringing self-fulfilment, then you are going to be disappointed – sooner or later. God has a better plan; it is that the two will become one flesh, the 'he and she' becomes 'us'. Mathematically it is expressed as 1+1=1. How *should* we frame the question then? Perhaps the best way of putting it is something like this: "At the moment I am one. I want to find a mate with whom I can become one, someone on whom I can lavish my love and affection so as to bring out the best in her, and she can bring out the best in me". Now this *bringing out the best* may or may not involve children. It is not essential to have children to enjoy a meaningful and successful married life, but (as we shall explore later) the biblical pattern is that God's intention is that children are the primary outcome of a 1+1 =1 relationship. Men and women, having become *one flesh* under God's blessing, are enabled to join with God in the creative process. God's creative purpose continues to this day – and we are part of it. God allows you and me to join Him in creation.

Straightaway I can hear some readers complain: how do procreative 'accidents' fit into this? What about men and women who have absolutely no intention of coming together "as one", and yet create children – where do they fit into this pattern? And more important, where do their (perhaps unwanted) children fit into this pattern? Others will ask: is God really so very interested in the minutiae of life that He feels it necessary to involve Himself in decisions as to which one (out of hundreds if not thousands of potential mates) I may actually choose? And yet other readers may be thinking that *certainly God does have in mind just the 'right' person* (for me, if not for everyone else) and He will cause the "coincidence" of meeting, romance, love and living happily ever after – and that I will "know" this rightness when I meet it. It will be seen, then, that there are many different approaches to this question of finding a *one flesh* mate. We come back to the question we posed in the Introduction to this book – do you want to live happily ever after? Do you want to live by the Maker's Instructions – or go your own way?

Let us come back to Adam and Eve: what principle in "courtship" do we discern in Genesis 2 and 3? God brought Eve to Adam. As we seek a *one flesh* mate, do we have a consciousness that God's hand is in this matter? Do we feel it necessary to manoeuvre circumstances, to chase, to flirt, to woo, or do we want to build on a better, a more solid foundation? God wants us to build upon a proper foundation – that is a key lesson we glean from Adam. His joy at meeting Eve is poignant as he exclaims: **"At last, here is one of my own kind. Bone taken from my bone, and flesh from my flesh. 'Woman' is her name because she was taken out of man."** Sensing the sheer joy that Adam has in meeting his mate, we see that his battle with loneliness is at an end. It is a wonderful testimony that many Christians have, that God brought them and their spouse together – and they had this conviction almost from day one!

A good friend of the author told him how he met his future wife at a Christian convention. He said that when he went he was conscious of being lonely and alone. He said that his prayer as he left to go to the convention was simply "Lord, may I find a special friend at this conference" – and this with no particular view of meeting God's intended. He met his special friend and she turned out to be very special indeed! They were married less than a year later. Neither of them worked particularly hard at the "finding" process – they just went to where they thought that God wanted them to be. He did the rest! Your author's experience in this matter was not quite so straightforward! Seeking a Christian mate became a priority. I kept my eyes open for "Miss Right" over a number of years. I gave God a helping hand wherever I felt He needed it – which seemed to be more often than I had expected! So I tried to make sure I was at the places where *the action* might be. And I thought that a suitable potential mate would quickly be introduced to the dubious charms of a very unknown Christian writer! If an introduction was not forthcoming then it was engineered, to give God that gentle nudge. Ironically, it was only when I stopped looking and left it with God that the action happened! There is an old saying: "Let go, and let God". In this matter of our finding His intended life partner this really seems to be the best possible advice. God does have a perfect plan and perfect timing.

Again I sense some readers will have immediate difficulties. They might well say, "I'm not a Christian, so where does that leave me?" Is God still interested in me and will He find me "Mr Right" or "Miss Right"? Yes, God is interested in you – whether or not you are presently a "Christian". But He can best help you to find His intended only to the extent that you co-operate with Him. Of course you can become a Christian at any time but please do not do so with any intention of using that as a vehicle to find a mate.

The reason for becoming a Christian is that you

recognise what Jesus has done for you and want to be His disciple forever. Recognising what He has done for you inevitably and rightly involves the emotional response of love – falling in love is too worldly a way of looking at it as people fall in and out of love – but there is a sense in which this is true. There will be a point at which you respond in repentance, trust and love. Other blessings undoubtedly do flow from being a Christian, including straightening out life's relationships and life's future, but the only legitimate reason for becoming a Christian is as a response to the love already shown to you personally – the love of the Father giving His Son for you – placing His Son in the place where you ought to have been. As we will return to that theme later in this book, we will leave it for now. Just bear in mind that a God who is love will indeed want for you the very best. Now the very best may not be your choice! Indeed the very best may be a surprise to you. Jesus said in Luke chapter 11:

Would any of you who are fathers give your son a snake when he asks for fish? Or would you give him a scorpion when he asks for an egg? As bad as you are, you know how to give good things to your children. How much more, then, will the Father in heaven give the Holy Spirit to those who ask him!"

Jesus was speaking specifically about the gift of the Holy Spirit, Who is promised to every true Believer, but the principle holds true for all God's gifts. God gives what is good. If you ask Him for what is good, then He will give it to you. It is as simple as that! If, as a disciple of Jesus, you are seeking a mate and you place the question with Him, then He will give you the best gift you could possibly want. Later in this book we will look a bit more at discerning the signs and being sure, but for now let's just rejoice in the knowledge that a loving Father has a great plan! When we offer these things to Him, He gives only the very best.

What Jesus taught about one flesh

So precisely when was it that Jesus spoke about this *one flesh* aspect of the relationship between man and woman? Crucially, He speaks about it in relation to divorce. We read much the same account in both Matthew 19: 1–12 and in Mark 10: 1–12. The context of Jesus' teaching is this: the Pharisees (religious diehards who hated Jesus and wanted to "fault" him before the religious authorities and the Roman authorities) thought they had a perfect wheeze with which to trap the Lord: get Him to take a clear position on the subject of divorce – then He would be bound to offend someone. (The same is true for His followers today). The political background to this trap was this: Herod, in whose realm Jesus was travelling, had divorced his wife in order to marry Herodias. He was very sensitive to any criticism – and indeed John the Baptist's death was occasioned in no small way by the fact that he openly criticised Herod's illegal "marriage" to Herodias. If diligent readers want to follow the sad and sleazy story then read Mark 6: 16–29 (also Matthew 14: 1–12). Divorce was a hot topic. So what would Jesus make of it?

Jewish opinion was sharply divided, so no matter what Jesus answered on the question of divorce, someone was bound to be upset, and those who opposed Him could well have thought He might end up in the same way as John the Baptist. The religious disciples of the Jewish theologian Hillel (who was a big noise in first century Judea – and has remained for Jews ever since a key Jewish Sage) believed that a man could divorce his wife when she became "disfavoured" in his eyes. Whilst some took "disfavour" to relate to the sin of adultery, others had more generous and liberal interpretations (from the man's point of view) and found a host of reasons why a man might get rid of his wife. If Jesus took a stringent viewpoint on the sanctity of marriage, then He would upset the followers of Hillel, as well as Herod the ruler. If Jesus took a "liberal" or "lenient" approach to marriage, then He would offend religious conservatives such as the Pharisees. How would Jesus respond?

Matthew 19: 3–12
Some Pharisees came to him and tried to trap him by asking, "Does our Law allow a man to divorce his wife for whatever reason he wishes?" Jesus answered, "Haven't you read the scripture that says that in the beginning the Creator made people male and female? And God said, 'For this reason a man will leave his father and mother and unite with his wife, and the two will become one.' So they are no longer two, but

one. No human being must separate, then, what God has joined together." The Pharisees asked him, "Why, then, did Moses give the law for a man to hand his wife a divorce notice and send her away?" Jesus answered, "Moses gave you permission to divorce your wives because you are so hard to teach. But it was not like that at the time of creation. I tell you, then, that any man who divorces his wife for any cause other than her unfaithfulness, commits adultery if he marries some other woman." His disciples said to him, "If this is how it is between a man and his wife, it is better not to marry." Jesus answered, "This teaching does not apply to everyone, but only to those to whom God has given it. For there are different reasons why men cannot marry: some, because they were born that way; others, because men made them that way; and others do not marry for the sake of the Kingdom of heaven. Let him who can accept this teaching do so."

Jesus has immediately come down on the "side" of the sanctity of marriage. There is no room for doubt as to His position, either then, or today! So who was offended? Certainly the followers of Hillel, certainly the Herodian party, certainly Herod himself. Whilst the Pharisees were pleased that Jesus had affirmed their high view of marriage, they were doubly pleased that He had been led to alienate some powerful enemies.

Jesus affirmed that it was "for this reason" that a man and woman would be joined as one. He was quoting the Bible of His day (what we call the Old Testament) and specifically Genesis 2: 24. As this is a key verse for this whole book, let's see it in two other translations:

NIV – "**For this reason a man will leave his father and mother and be united with his wife, and the two will become one flesh**."

RSV – "**Therefore a man leaves his father and mother and cleaves to his wife, and they become one flesh**."

Without wanting to be unduly focused on words, let us just focus on "for this reason" (NIV) and "therefore" (RSV) for a moment. These words are foundational and central to the arguments explored throughout this book, so the effort here will certainly be well rewarded later! Genesis 2: 24 tells us that the two are united as a single flesh *for a reason*. Jesus affirmed that. So what was this reason? Genesis suggests that it is because the two are already one – Eve is created from the essence of Adam. Every child ever born is created from the essence of a man and a woman, so each and every one of us carries within us this reality. We are made up, whether male or female, of X and Y chromosomes. Even within ourselves we are one flesh, albeit that in each case one set of chromosomes is dominant and so we are recognisably male or female. Because of this, a man will leave his father and mother and "cleave to" his wife.

Because we live in an "equality" driven postmodern world, we subconsciously bring our own agendas to bear as we consider this. Once again some fairly obvious "objections" are going to leap out. For very many –

especially in the Western world – this rite of leaving simply does not happen in practice. Because of extended Further or Higher Education, or the need to work away from home, or the simple gratification of "flying the nest" and setting up on their own, most young people in the West no longer mark an obvious and definite "leaving" and so deny themselves the rite of *leaving and cleaving*. Once again, we will tease out these thoughts more fully later in the book. But for now we will affirm this: Jesus looked back to the Scriptures as they were given and He clearly affirmed them. There was no obfuscation. God's revealed word was quite adequate for Jesus. Why would it be inadequate for us?

But Jesus went further than just affirming the words. He brought to life the meaning behind them. Having "cleaved", the two are no longer two but are one. 1+1=1. What God has joined should not be "put asunder", to use the old fashioned language of the English church's traditional marriage rite. "**Man must not separate what God has joined together**" (Matthew 19: 6). Jesus had now added the Scriptural command, the Scriptural law, that man cannot interfere with what God has already done. BUT... once again the 'rubber hits the road' on this question. There is a circumstance in which, reluctantly, God allows men and women to put asunder what He has put together. That one cause is marital unfaithfulness – to be blunt it is having sex with someone other than your spouse.

And why did God give this "permission" to divorce? Was it so that the wronged partner could *get their own back* – to take revenge? Was it so they could get half the family estate (the legal practice in most Western countries today)? Was it so that the wronged partner might once again be "free" to enjoy the benefits of a new *one flesh* relationship – this time with someone who might be fully trusted? No. This permission was granted, "because you are so hard to teach". The Lord Jesus is not affirming divorce as a right. It is a wrong in all circumstances but one – and even then it is only available as an option because we have hard hearts. Rather than tearing apart what God has placed together, we should be seeking to repair the damage, restore the oneness and fully forgive so that the two might once more move forward in unity.

Now once again, dear reader, I sense hackles rising and tears welling. I would simply ask you to *stay with it* for now. There is good news ahead, but we need to get the foundations clear before we can build an enduring structure. If we find Jesus' teaching uncomfortable, we are not the only ones. Look at what His disciples said (verse 10) **"If this is how it is between a man and his wife, it is better not to marry."** They too were perplexed. If a man might be insulted and cuckolded (to use a really old-fashioned word – look it up in a dictionary if you are unfamiliar with it) in a decidedly patriarchal society, and be denied the "right" to divorce (remember Jesus has just taken away their "right" which never actually existed in fact and He has replaced it with a bitter concession **"because you are so hard to teach"**) then why marry at all? It is surely better not to marry!

We immediately see the hardness of heart of these

disciples. They wanted the "right" to get even. Perhaps some of them were secret admirers of the Hillel position, that a man should have the right to divorce his wife as and when she met with his disfavour – for any reason. Surely these men *were* hard of heart!

The author's wife is a seamstress of no mean capability. She tells me that if in making a dress or some other item, having joined together different sub-sections of the whole, there is a reason to separate them, then it is impossible to do it without leaving damage to the fabric, even if it is possible to hide that damage from the human eye. What has been joined cannot be un-joined without irreparable damage. Functionality may be restored when the piece is finished, damage may be hidden, but it remains there forever. Even where we have the right to divorce, the damage to the individuals remains – one reason why we are to be very careful how we choose our life's partner in the first place.

So Jesus affirmed scripture and affirmed the sanctity of marriage. This has been the church's position down through history until the present day. It is only today, in our post-Christian culture which seems to be spawning a post-Christian church, that the church seems unable any more to offer clear guidance. The guidance of much of the church today sounds more like that of an agony aunt than a clarion echo of the voice of God. Jesus' teaching on divorce was by no means all He had to say about relationships and marriage. But there is an intriguing conclusion to this discussion in the Gospel of Matthew. See again verses 11 and 12. Here the Good News Bible's translation is not altogether helpful: **"This teaching does not apply to everyone, but only to those to whom God has given it. For there are different reasons why men cannot marry: some, because they were born that way; others, because men made them that way; and others do not marry for the sake of the Kingdom of heaven. Let him who can accept this teaching do so."**

At a casual glance this paraphrase might be mistaken as meaning that the teaching on divorce is optional *because it does not apply to everyone*. What Jesus is in fact saying is that the teaching that a man shall leave his parents and cleave to his wife does not apply to everyone.

Whilst relationship-forming and marriage are clearly the pattern that God has established for most men and women, it is not for everyone. Jesus himself did not "leave and cleave". There are three categories of person for whom marriage will not be an option. Some have no interest in marriage because they were born that way. The word Jesus actually used is "eunuch". Someone born a eunuch is someone who has no sexual drive – and surprising as it may be to our sex-obsessed age, there *are* perfectly healthy people who have no such interest. Eunuchs can be made – in the ancient world and right up to the end of the Ottoman Empire, some were castrated for cultural reasons. Plainly they could not *leave and cleave* to a wife. Does our modern culture create "eunuchs"? Finally, there are those who deny themselves the right to marry "for the sake of the kingdom". Down through history, many missionaries and others called out by God to special and sanctified service, recognise that marriage will divert them from kingdom work and so accept the personal sacrifice of not marrying and not seeing their own children. Not many are called to such sacrifice, but some definitely are – and Jesus specifically affirmed them. We should affirm them too.

So we conclude this chapter. Jesus was emphatic that the Scriptures are right – God has created us male and female and *for this reason* God created us – to enjoy each other, to defeat loneliness and to have the joy of sharing with God in the creative process. We need to keep this *one flesh* dynamic in mind throughout this book as we explore God's purposes more fully and as we consider some of the very real and very practical questions around forming and sustaining relationships. We have certainly not answered every question about two becoming one, for example: precisely when do we become *one flesh*? When we meet? When we marry? When we mate? Or the question: can we become *one flesh* with more than one person? Answers to these questions will become more apparent as we explore further what Jesus taught.

"Happy are those who have been invited to the wedding feast"

2

BOY MEETS GIRL

Two Halves or One Whole?

There is just so much in the Bible that relates to men, women, relationships and marriage. We are going to have to limit ourselves to consider a few examples in detail. To look at everything would make this book unduly long and difficult! So what are the key questions that a reader might have, now that we have considered this *one flesh* dynamic that is so central to God's perfect plan for men and women? We really do need to bring this book, with its necessary emphasis on the teachings of the Lord Jesus, right down to practical applications – ones that will help us through the real life day-to-day questions we must face.

But we do so in the belief that the lessons we pick up in the Bible still hold true today, and that these are lessons we can apply to our own times and to our own lives. We come back to the Toulouse incident mentioned in the Introduction. God has a great plan for us, if only we are prepared to let Him be God of our lives – and our loves. He has set it all down in writing, but to take advantage of it we need to read it, mark it, learn it, apply it. If we cannot be bothered to do that, then we are courting disaster. If you want to form a wonderful *one flesh* relationship and enjoy all its blessings, then at the very minimum you are going to need to do a little bit of work to seek the Maker's mind in this. If you cannot be bothered, then perhaps you are not in reality too fussed about what sort of relationship you will eventually form and are prepared to take a chance on it.

The killer questions for each one of us are these:

How should I pick my lifetime partner?

Perhaps that should be how should I *identify* my lifetime's partner – moving us away from the slightly selfish idea that we get *a pick*, or we aim to get *the pick of the bunch*, towards the idea that there is a wonderful partner out there and we are going to use our best resources to identify him or her, and to honour him or her by our attitude now, even before we have met.

How should our relationship be founded?

How will it begin? How will we know it has begun?

What will be our mutual objectives as we consider the prospect of becoming one flesh?

Do we need objectives or do we allow 'love' to carry us through?

How far may we/should we go in our physical relationship...

...as we get to know each other and as we try to discern the viability of the relationship we are trying to build?

We might add to that: should we be thinking in terms of a quick courtship, or a long, deliberative process? Does a quick courtship necessarily mean we do not sufficiently know each other, because we have not had the opportunity to see each other in a range of representative situations that will bring out the best, and the worst, for all to see, and is this necessary? Similarly, and in reverse, does a long courtship help us to achieve the assurance we definitely want and need? And can even such an extended courtship ever provide a sufficient range of experiences so that we can say we "know" our partner intimately?

These are real and weighty questions. May we really hope that a book – the Bible, written at its most recent some two thousand years ago – can help us today? Assuming that He exists, does God really mind how we go about this courtship process so long as we reach the right answer? Then, if we try to do all of this in a biblically focused way, are we in danger of spoiling the fun of romance, and the thrill of the chase? Are we like the proverbial scientist, pulling the wings off a butterfly to see how it works? Surely this little thing called "chemistry" is what it is all about? People know when they are in love and surely that is all that matters?

Yes, to analyse and theorise about love and romance may be to take the "fun" out of it, but maybe we should consider that the issues at stake are just too important to do it any other way. If we are *designed* (and I use that word with its full weight and its full implication!) to benefit from a *one flesh* relationship, then to risk establishing that relationship with the wrong person – and that's what it may simply boil down to – is to take an enormous gamble with our lives, with our happiness, with the happiness of our partner, and of any children who result from the relationship. Heavy responsibilities!

The Bible gives us no indication at all that there is only *one* person in all eternity that we might marry. A very modern idea is that of a *soul mate*. It is significant that in two thousand years of preparation, the Bible in no place so much hints at such an idea. The modern idea owes much to the so-called New Age movement, but a quick Google (e.g. Wikipedia) will display the full pagan roots of the concept. What the Bible's silence means in practice is extremely liberating! It means that in principle I can find happiness with any one of many people, perhaps innumerable people, providing both I and my chosen partner are prepared to work at it as we build our lives together. It also means that if we make a "mistake" about whom we choose, there is no ultimate reason why that mistake cannot be corrected as we move through life together. This again suggests we have to work at the relationship, to preserve it, to nurture it, to protect it. But relationships that get off to a shaky start can still be very fulfilling and fully successful. That's what we sometimes call *God's economy*! That's God's way of doing things! He can turn mistakes into triumphs!

It is liberating in another way, too. If my wife thought that God had planned me from the very beginning of time to be *the one and only*, just meant for her, and meant for no one else, then I think she could legitimately (if reverently) complain that He might have done a better job, because Peter Sammons isn't perfect – in fact he's a very long way from it. My wife might feel thoroughly devalued by any such idea that I was the one and only in the whole universe, and marked out from the beginning of time as her "other half"!

None of what we have said so far suggests that God is uninterested in whom we choose, nor that He does not, in fact, have a wonderful and special choice just for me (and you!) But this is a million miles away from the new-agey, semi-religious, semi-pagan idea of a soul mate, floating around the spiritual ether just waiting to be hooked-up to a *Mr* or to a *Miss Mate*. No, the biblical reality is much more interesting and much more exciting than that. We humans are made in the likeness of God (Genesis 1: 26). Whether male or female we have similar aspirations, similar needs, and the same spiritual make-up, whether or not we acknowledge God. Let us use a quick analogy from the workplace. No one in their right mind says, "I simply cannot work with this team, I must work within a team made for me in heaven, of entirely perfect, entirely compatible co-workers. And I won't take any job until I find the perfect team!" In working life we just recognise differences, make allowances for them and get on with the job. In exactly the same way there are many people with whom we might theoretically become *one flesh* and build a perfectly satisfactory *one flesh* relationship. It is not ultimately the particular individual that counts, with all their foibles and weaknesses, but it is the willingness to recognise and the determination to preserve that *one flesh* relationship that is the true key to success or failure.

Two halves or one whole? Without wishing to be bogged-down into a sort of mathematical philosophy, the Bible does not teach that 0.5+0.5=1, as though all those who are not in a *one flesh* relationship are somehow "incomplete". There is assuredly a place for singleness in God's economy, and in some respects that status is exalted in the Bible, as providing for some a passport to dedicated kingdom-building service. (See 1 Corinthians 7 if you want to see the Apostle Paul's view on marriage and singleness). So, before were are brought together and become one, we were not incomplete – we were not half a person! We repeat that in God's economy the pattern is 1+1=1.

So, boy meets girl. Boy and girl recognise possibilities and 'court' each other to see if those possibilities are likely to be realised in practice. We will leave for the time being the question of whether marriage is the only way that a meaningful relationship can be expressed. The idea of courtship is a particularly Western one. We note that in many cultures the concept of the "arranged marriage" predominates. A young man and a young woman may have little real choice or influence in the matter. People who believe in these cultural norms say that they lead to perfectly satisfactory relationships. Whether we agree with the idea of arranged marriages or not, the fact that they exist and often seem to be the basis for satisfactory mutually supportive relationships does also seem to confirm the idea that there are actually innumerable people with whom one might find happiness (or a measure of happiness) and that the "soul mate" concept is simply unreal. There is a real poignancy to this idea of courtship, however. If, having "courted", one or even both parties conclude that there is no future in the relationship, then it breaks. Almost inevitably, someone gets hurt – often deeply. Is this *really* God's way?

The Bible does have some clear pointers to how to go about finding a mate. Having established the creation ordinance in Genesis – that two will become one (or 1+1=1 as we have put it), so through the Bible we see the different ways in which the creation ordinance can be worked out in practice. The Bible teaches us two things about *one flesh* relationships: first, how they can be formed in the first place; and, second, how, once they have been formed, they can be trashed or exalted, depending on how we behave. We return in Chapter 4 to the biblical pattern for marriage. But we now explore the biblical account of Isaac and Rebecca's meeting, to see what this can tell us about successful and healthy – or deeply flawed – relationships.

Isaac and Rebecca – True Love

The point is well made that true love between a man and a woman is not mentioned in the Bible until we reach Isaac and Rebecca, in Genesis chapter 24. (As the story is a long one, you may want to read the whole of that chapter.) It is a rather lovely story of romance, as well as a story of what today we can only call an arranged marriage. In essence, Abraham wants his son Isaac to have a wife and sends his oldest (and presumably wisest) servant to find him one. Abraham does not want that wife to be a Canaanite, but rather that she should be from the land that Abraham had left when he was called by God to go to Canaan. Abraham does not want Isaac to return to the land of his forefathers to assist the search – quite why is unclear, but perhaps he thought that Isaac would be tempted to settle there with his new wife and so God's purposes in bringing Abraham and his descendents to their *promised land* would be defeated. So the wife would be brought to Isaac. In this we see a faint echo of God bringing Eve to Adam – there is a pattern being established here – that God will be delighted to bring to each one us the mate of His choosing, which will be the very best mate for us.

Having received his instructions from Abraham, the unnamed servant took ten camels and travelled to a place called Nahor, which was probably located in Modern Iraq. He prayed for inspiration as he looked for the right woman. We take up the story:

Genesis 24: 12–24
He prayed, "Lord, God of my master Abraham, give me success today and keep your promise to my master. Here I am at the well where the young women of the city will be coming to get water. I will say to one of them, 'Please, lower your jar and let me have a drink.' If she says, 'Drink, and I will also bring water for your camels,' may she be the one that you have chosen for your servant Isaac. If this happens, I will know that you have kept your promise to my master."

Before he had finished praying, Rebecca arrived with a water jar on her shoulder. She was the daughter of Bethuel, who was the son of Abraham's brother Nahor and his wife Milcah. She was a very beautiful young woman and still a virgin. She went down to the well, filled her jar, and came back. The servant ran to meet her and said, "Please give me a drink of water from your jar." She said, "Drink, sir," and quickly lowered her jar from her shoulder and held it while he drank. When he had finished, she said, "I will also bring water for your camels and let them have all they want." She quickly emptied her jar into the animals' drinking trough and ran to the well to get more water, until she had watered all his camels. The man kept watching her in silence, to see if the Lord had given him success. When she had finished, the man took an expensive gold ring and put it in her nose and put two large gold bracelets on her arms. He said, "Please tell me who your father is. Is there room in his house for my men and me to spend the night?"

"My father is Bethuel son of Nahor and Milcah," she answered.

The servant leaves the matter with God. He sets out a detailed and faithful request. In essence: please show me who the right girl is, and I will recognise the signs by her behaviour. Whilst the servant's specific approach, setting out a detailed plan, may or may not be right for us as individuals, the principle certainly is. If we want to make a choice that accords with God's will (which is always good), then we have to make space for Him act for us. Having handed the problem over to God, we will surely recognise the signs when He answers our prayer.

Having had his prayer answered very quickly, directly and in a way that left him full of confidence, the servant had identified the right girl, and he thanked God joyfully. We pick up the account again at the point where the servant is speaking with Rebecca's father – soon to be Isaac's father-in-law.

Genesis 24: 48–67

"Now, if you intend to fulfil your responsibility toward my master and treat him fairly, please tell me; if not, say so, and I will decide what to do." Laban and Bethuel answered, "Since this matter comes from the Lord, it is not for us to make a decision. Here is Rebecca; take her and go. Let her become the wife of your master's son, as the Lord himself has said." When the servant of Abraham heard this, he bowed down and worshiped the Lord. Then he brought out clothing and silver and gold jewelry, and gave them to Rebecca. He also gave expensive gifts to her brother and to her mother. Then Abraham's servant and the men with him ate and drank, and spent the night there. When they got up in the morning, he said, "Let me go back to my master."

But Rebecca's brother and her mother said, "Let her stay with us a week or ten days, and then she may go." But he said, "Don't make us stay. The Lord has made my journey a success; let me go back to my

master." They answered, "Let's call her and find out what she has to say." So they called Rebecca and asked, "Do you want to go with this man?"

"Yes," she answered. So they let Rebecca and her old family servant go with Abraham's servant and his men. And they gave Rebecca their blessing in these words: "May you, sister, become the mother of millions! May your descendants conquer the cities of their enemies!"

Then Rebecca and her young women got ready and mounted the camels to go with Abraham's servant, and they all started out. Isaac had come into the wilderness of "The Well of the Living One Who Sees Me" and was staying in the southern part of Canaan. He went out in the early evening to take a walk in the fields and saw camels coming.

When Rebecca saw Isaac, she got down from her camel and asked Abraham's servant, "Who is that man walking toward us in the field?"

"He is my master," the servant answered. So she took her scarf and covered her face. The servant told Isaac everything he had done. Then Isaac brought Rebecca into the tent that his mother Sarah had lived in, and she became his wife. Isaac loved Rebecca, and so he was comforted for the loss of his mother."

The godly principles suggested above are these: *Firstly* we can and should allow God the space to make the choice for us. Whilst we have already noted that in reality we might enjoy a perfectly wholesome *one flesh* relationship with potentially many alternatives, in reality God has in mind for us the very best person – His choice! This very best person is a million miles away from the world's ideas of "soul mates", but still we can be deeply grateful that God has in mind His very best choice and He will make that choice real to us – if we allow Him.

Secondly, although this was an arranged marriage there is no implication that all marriages should be arranged. Far from it! And indeed there are other patterns of courtship displayed in the Bible, as we shall see later. Although "arranged", the bride-to-be Rebecca was given final say over the precise timing of her departure. We sense all through this account that Rebecca is a willing party to the marriage – her 'sovereignty' has not been denied, rather she works with her family and, allowing that this was the marriage of a key person in God's *salvation story*, it could well be that Rebecca sensed somehow God's hand upon her life and the rightness of the offer made to her. We also sense that, like Mary the mother of Jesus, Rebecca also had the right to reject God's choice for her life, but chose to go with His plan.

Thirdly and finally, we mark the fact that Isaac loved his new wife. With arranged marriages, and a totally patriarchal society, men were not necessarily expected to have any *phileo* love for their wives – and yet Isaac did. Like Adam, Isaac was bowled over with God's choice and fell in love. No doubt the love modified and settled down in due course but we can only smile at the happy thought that Isaac and Rebecca enjoyed the love that we call 'romantic'!

All You Need Is Love!

Now we can share a thought that will be shockingly strange to many – indeed I would venture to say to most – people who live in the cultures of the West! It is this: love is not the basis for marriage, so much as marriage is the basis for love. This may be to overstate the case somewhat, but please bear with me! Notice the order of Genesis 24: 67 – **Isaac brought Rebecca into the tent that his mother Sarah had lived in, and she became his wife. Isaac loved Rebecca, and so he was comforted for the loss of his mother.** We remember how the Apostle Paul in the New Testament said (Ephesians 5: 25) "**Husbands, love your wives just as Christ loved the church and gave his life for it**". Paul's instruction was to love your wife, not your intended. The emphasis on love when found in the Bible is generally after marriage, rather than before it. This is not to suggest that love before marriage is unimportant, but perhaps here we are faced with the blunt reality that any fool can "fall in love", but it takes real effort to stay in love. That is the sort of love that God desires for His people. The love we find in Scripture is not the hormone-charged variety so favoured in the world at large, a mixture of soap-opera emotion that hovers close to infatuation, and downright lust. The Bible's love is not that 'love' that fills the broadcast air waves in romantic love songs and poetry. It really does seem that the more that the world pursues this type of 'love', sings about it and makes endless feature films about it, the higher the divorce rate becomes. Plainly, this 'love' is not the glue that holds marriages together.

It is *commitment* rather than 'love' that holds together a marriage. This is an unbreakable and unconditional commitment that is made before God as two take each other to become husband and wife, in a 1+1=1 relationship. In this we mark forever the leaving and especially the cleaving dynamic of the male and female journey. What is the bottom line here? What all this means in practice is that couples are not able to just walk away from a marriage if they discover that 'love' is gone. There can be no defence of "I don't love her any more." Only within the commitment of marriage can love truly flourish. It is only when I have the security of an indissoluble relationship that I can allow myself to be known by my spouse. Without that security I cannot risk being understood. And if I cannot take that risk I will never know the oneness of which Genesis speaks and which Jesus affirmed.

This becomes the classic argument of marriage versus cohabitation (or 'shacking up' as the Americans have it). If you truly love each other, then why not marry? If you don't know that you truly love each other, then why cohabit as a sham mimic of marriage? We revert to the vexed question of cohabitation in a *one flesh* context in chapter 6. If a couple should tragically reach the conclusion that they do not now have the "love" for one another that they once thought they had, and so should never have married, then what are they to do? The Bible is emphatic – the husband must love his wife. God has commanded it so it must be possible! We have to learn to love in that way.

I am indebted to A J Higgins, an American Christian writer, for some of the thoughts in this section. Higgins wrote a great little book, mainly for Christian young people, called *Marriage and The Family* (Gospel Tract Publications, 1988, ISBN 0948417293). Higgins makes this key point: the secular world at large has popularised the idea that somehow "love" enables couples to conquer problems – but the truth is that marriage actually magnifies problems – as does cohabitation, in fact. We learn from Isaac and Rebecca that, in marriage, God has prepared a soil in which love can grow to its fullest potential, but this is only possible when both man and woman recognise the permanency of their commitment.

Hopefully readers will not by now be forming the suspicion or opinion that commitment in the *one flesh* sense planned by God is simply impossible to achieve. It is possible but it is hard! We need to develop a mature attitude to relationships as we plan for our future. You only get one life to live, so it is as best to try to live it as well as possible. God promises His help if you ask Him BUT... "Toulouse" or "To Lose"? It is back to the question in the Introduction to this book. The Maker's Instructions are available and in principle can be followed by all. So what is stopping us?

The key thing that is stopping us is our rebellious nature. When God sets out limits on behaviour we almost always bridle at the limitation. Inevitably we want to be "god" over our own lives and run things our own way. We are inveterate rebels when it comes to God and His rules. Lack of space prevents us from exploring fully "The Fall" as described in Genesis chapter 3, when Eve and Adam decided to ignore the Maker's Instruction and "eat" the one fruit that was forbidden to them. But the reality is there for all to see – for each and every one of us, whether male or female, Jew or Gentile, we rebel against God's holy requirements, in spite of the love that He bears towards us.

All you need is love, say the pop singers and film makers. Perhaps they are right. Perhaps they are wrong! But we can usefully modify that statement by saying All You Need is God's Love. Or round it off completely and say: All You Need is God's love and God's Power. As we think about our love life and our life partner, we certainly can hand things over to God in the way that Isaac did, in the expectation that He will identify for us our loved one. But, I venture to suggest, only in the context of a love relationship with God. The love of God already displayed to us should be given back to Him and only within that love relationship we can learn to trust Him with guiding us towards our *one flesh* partner. We should avoid a "slot machine" mentality on this. We seek to follow Jesus (that's what a love relationship with God actually means) not simply so He will oblige us by doing nice things for us – like finding us a suitable wife or husband. But we can be assured that as we follow Jesus, so we will learn more of God's purposes and this whole area of mate-finding will become easier for us.

At this point we need to renew the challenge: if you are serious about finding the right person just for you, then what adjustments to your behaviour are you prepared to make? Are you prepared to honour your partner now, whom you might not yet even have met – and may not meet for some years? Are you prepared to work to God's timing (which is always perfect!) or are you in an unholy rush? We began this chapter with some killer questions that virtually all people have in regard to their love lives. Hopefully, as we explore what Jesus taught about love, marriage, relationships and sex, we will finally get a real insight into how God wants us to interact with each other – and with Him.

> *"Happy are those who have been invited*
> *to the wedding feast"*

3

THE SONG OF SONGS

The Old Liar

In chapters 1 and 2 we introduced this idea of *one flesh*. Let's summarise the thoughts in those chapters and draw out a few conclusions.

God created us with a good purpose in mind. He created us in His own (spiritual) image. Male and female were created with the basic objective of being given to each other. By being given to each other, men and women can enter into a *one flesh* relationship. We will go on exploring the idea of *one flesh* throughout this book, but hopefully by now we at least understand it is something very precious and it is God's gift to us. We can say definitely:

God made us male and female for a reason;
Because God made us He cares about us;
Because God is love, He desires the best for us;
God has in mind for us the best possible mate – someone with whom we can and should be happy;
The Maker designed us to be complemented by each other.

On this last point and just to be clever with words, God designed us to be *complemented* by each other, and be complimented by each other! This idea of compliments brings us neatly to The Song of Songs, which is the book of the Old Testament (one aspect of which might be termed the "Promise" as suggested in our Introduction) that speaks uniquely about romantic love. If God has in mind for most (not all) of us the joy of a *one flesh* relationship, we need to note that God's enemy – whom the Bible calls the Devil, or Satan – has a singular objective of spoiling that relationship. We will not waste time in considering who this spiritual being called Satan is, except to note that Jesus encountered him as a real and personal enemy (Matthew 4: 1–11; Mark 1: 12–13; Luke 4: 1–13; John 8: 42–47). If Jesus encountered him as this type of enemy, then we will as well. Jesus said of him "**From the very beginning he was a murderer and has never been on the side of truth, because there is no truth in him. When he tells a lie, he is only doing what is natural to him, because he is a liar and the father of lies**" (John 8: 44). We are warned by Jesus to be alert for this enemy, and to resist him (e.g. James 4: 7). Once again some readers may have issues and difficulties with this idea of Satan, but Christians take their lead from Jesus on this. For those who do not presently believe in the reality of Satan, you are invited to switch on your TV news channel tonight and see the evidence, sadly all too clear. There is something devilishly wrong with our world.

As we consider God's designs for love, romance and marriage, let's keep in mind that key statement made by Jesus about the devil, teaching us that the devil is **a liar and the father of lies**. As we look at the whole area of sexual temptation we need to keep in mind this idea of a *lie*. Those things which are harmful to us are often presented as being a pleasure that we are being denied, or are denying to ourselves. And where do lies come from? We need to retain that thought in the back of our minds. Every untruth comes from the devil. Any good biblical commentary will show how the devil's temptation of Eve and Adam was founded on the use of lies in order to get Eve – and then Adam – to do what God had specifically told them not to do (see Genesis Chapter 3). The same is too often true in the area of sexual temptation. God has given a clear instruction that two will become one, and that is beneficial for their own blessing and for the blessing of society. But the world's lie (if you like) is to say that one should be united with as many as possible, so as to bring physical pleasure and a different sort of emotional fulfilment. In the same way that Eve was willing to go along with the lie, so we too are all too often minded to go along with the lie, because it is attractive.

Plato and Augustine

The most recent parts of the Bible are nearly two thousand years old. The earliest parts of the Bible precede the latest by about one and a half thousand years. Can such an ancient document really be used as a guide to help us through life in this third millennium? If I am keen to meet my intended, my life's mate and to settle down, can a pre-Iron Age book really show me what's right and what's wrong today? Christians would say an emphatic 'yes' to this question, no matter how odd that may seem to some people. "**The Word of God is alive and active, sharper than any two-edged sword. It cuts all the way through, to where soul and spirit meet .... it judges the desires and thoughts of man's heart**" (Hebrews 4: 12). The Bible itself tells us that it is "alive" and "active". As a living book it speaks to living people – in all ages and all cultures.

As suggested in the Introduction to this book, the way the Bible speaks to us will be affected by the way that we read the book: for these studies we try to read it in its plainest and most literal sense, unless the context is clearly demanding some other way in which it should be understood. The mind we try to apply is the mind that we believe Jesus would have applied to the scriptures of His day (i.e. what we call the Old Testament), using a Hebrew mindset rather than a Greek mindset. A Hebraic mindset tends to be more 'liberal' in interpreting than the cold, logical 'Greek' mind we have inherited from our classical Greek-influenced Western culture. The point is rightly made that a great deal of Greek philosophy found its way into the early church and has dominated its thinking ever since. There is no evidence that Jesus was in any way influenced by Greek philosophy, and he maintained throughout His life a truly Hebraic mind. But Greek philosophy has definitely influenced the way we all consider love, relationships and sex.

There are two characters in history who have had an arguably deleterious effect on the way the church uses its collective mind – although in saying this the author is aware he will 'make enemies' along the way! Plato was a Greek philosopher of the fourth century BC. At the risk of grossly over simplifying, Plato thought that the physical realm, as he understood it, was bad and that the non-physical realm was good, and that the two realms were in permanent conflict with each other. The physical realm is, of course, the one we all live in now – and in which we might hope to enjoy a *one flesh* relationship with our mate. Plato had what can only be called a low view of physical love. Indeed it is this low view that gives us the idea of "Platonic love" – a spiritual love without physical expression. Jump forward nine hundred odd years and we reach Augustine of Hippo – a Christian philosopher and theologian who was heavily influenced by Platonism. Augustine had led a dissolute life in his youth and blamed his physical body, which he thought led him to sinful actions. So he also had a low view of sexual expression, seeing it almost as a concession within marriage to otherwise sinful and unhealthy desires.

So why are we looking at the attitudes of two very ancient philosophers to understand what the Bible teaches about love, relationships, marriage and sex? We are looking because it is vital to understand that the church's teaching has been heavily dominated by Greek philosophy and, where the church has sounded confused in its teaching on sex and relationships, we need to remind ourselves that the church's mindset (Greek) is significantly different from its Lord's mindset (Jesus' mindset) which is unquestionably Hebrew. What God created was good. In Genesis chapter 1 most English language translations state seven times that what God created was good. Here the slight paraphrase of the Good News Bible is deficient – it simply says seven times that God was "pleased" with what He had made. But this is to miss the point altogether; what God made was (and is) fundamentally good. Because what God made was good, we can conclude quite happily that sexual expression of love is also fundamentally good. That's how God designed it!

What God made was (and is) good, until it was spoiled by man's sin in going his own way – disobeying the Maker's Instructions. Physical love is also fundamentally good until it is spoiled by mankind's determination to do things his own way, against the Maker's Instructions. Follow the Maker's Instructions and joy is the outcome. Ignore the Maker's Instructions and sooner or later tragedy strikes. Later in this book we will draw out precisely what are the Maker's Instructions regarding physical love and the context in which it is to be experienced and enjoyed. But in this chapter we focus on the fact that the Bible is not "prudish" about the subject of romantic love, nor the wholesome anticipation of physical love. Whilst we find clues to this non-prudishness throughout the Bible (if we are minded to look for it), it becomes most explicit in the Song of Songs, to which we now turn our attention.

The Song of Solomon

The Song of Songs, also known as the Song of Solomon, is a series of love poems. A short book – only eight chapters – it contains only poetry. The Song of Songs (like the book of Esther) does not mention God at all. For the most part the poems in The Song are addressed by a man to a woman and, in reply, by the woman to the man. They are like an exchange of love letters in poetic form. We have to wonder what joys modern young people miss by not exchanging love letters! Somehow texts and e-mails don't really cut the mustard as regards expressing love. The same is true of married couples – how infrequently do we write love letters, thinking that our regular contact on a day to day basis is all that's required! There really is an art to keeping romance alive.

Some people will argue that the Song of Songs is not really a love letter and is not really about romantic love. In reality, they say, it is a letter of love from Christ to His church (or if they are Jewish, they will say it is a letter of love from Yahweh to the Hebrew people). I will risk making more enemies by saying that this is almost certainly wrong on both counts! Others point out that the book is steamy to the point of eroticism, and that many Christians in particular, are frankly embarrassed by it. In some thirty-three years of Christian life, this author has heard only one sermon preached from The Song! It is almost certainly true to say that the vast bulk of the church, whether Eastern Orthodox, Roman Catholic, or Protestant, read the Song of Solomon with a Greek mindset, seeing romantic love and the anticipation of physical love as somehow naughty, or even dirty. A Hebraic mind would have less difficulty with this, and I would reverently suggest that our Lord as a Hebrew untainted with Platonism or Greek philosophy of any sort, would also have seen The Song in its plainest possible meaning.

Readers are encouraged to read the whole eight chapters to see the artlessness and honesty with which the lovers anticipate each other. We will sample only a few representative extracts here, but the whole is worth reading, even though the language is foreign to our way of thinking. Whilst the imagery is foreign, the powerful emotion behind the language is quite inescapable. A modern English translation will be most helpful, and once again I will recommend the Good News Bible as being easy to understand.

To see how artless the book is we turn straight to Chapter 1 as the woman begins her love song:

Woman to Man – Song of Songs 1: 2 – 3
Your lips cover me with kisses; your love is better than wine. There is a fragrance about you; the sound of your name recalls it. No woman could keep from loving you. Take me with you, and we'll run away; be my king and take me to your room. We will be happy together, drink deep, and lose ourselves in love. No wonder all women love you!

Man to Woman – Song of Songs 1: 9–11

You, my love, excite men as a mare excites the stallions of Pharaoh's chariots. Your hair is beautiful upon your cheeks and falls along your neck like jewels. But we will make for you a chain of gold with ornaments of silver.

Woman to Man – Song of Songs 1: 12–14

My king was lying on his couch, and my perfume filled the air with fragrance. My lover has the scent of myrrh as he lies upon my breasts. My lover is like the wild flowers that bloom in the vineyards at Engedi.

Woman to Man – Song of Songs 2: 3–7

Like an apple tree among the trees of the forest, so is my dearest compared to other men. I love to sit in its shadow, and its fruit is sweet to my taste. He brought me to his banquet hall and raised the banner of love over me. Restore my strength with raisins and refresh me with apples! I am weak from passion. His left hand is under my head, and his right hand caresses me. Promise me, women of Jerusalem; swear by the swift deer and the gazelles that you will not interrupt our love.

Man to Woman – Song of Songs 2: 10–14

My lover speaks to me. Come then, my love; my darling, come with me. The winter is over; the rains have stopped; in the countryside the flowers are in bloom. This is the time for singing; the song of doves is heard in the fields. Figs are beginning to ripen; the air is fragrant with blossoming vines. Come then, my love; my darling, come with me. You are like a dove that hides in the crevice of a rock. Let me see your lovely face and hear your enchanting voice.

Woman to Man – Song of Songs 2: 16–3: 5

My lover is mine, and I am his. He feeds his flock among the lilies until the morning breezes blow and the darkness disappears. Return, my darling, like a gazelle, like a stag on the mountains of Bether.

Asleep on my bed, night after night I dreamed of the one I love; I was looking for him, but couldn't find him. I went wandering through the city, through its streets and alleys. I looked for the one I love. I looked, but couldn't find him. The sentries patrolling the city saw me. I asked them, "Have you found my lover?" As soon as I left them, I found him. I held him and wouldn't let him go until I took him to my mother's house, to the room where I was born. Promise me, women of Jerusalem; swear by the swift deer and the gazelles that you will not interrupt our love.

Man to Woman – Song of Songs 4: 9–11

The look in your eyes, my sweetheart and bride, and the necklace you are wearing have stolen my heart. Your love delights me, my sweetheart and bride. Your love is better than wine; your perfume more fragrant than any spice. The taste of honey is on your lips, my darling; your tongue is milk and honey for me. Your clothing has all the fragrance of Lebanon.

Between the Man and the Woman – Song of Songs 5: 2–6

The Woman

While I slept, my heart was awake. I dreamed my lover knocked at the door.

The Man

Let me come in, my darling, my sweetheart, my dove. My head is wet with dew, and my hair is damp from the mist.

The Woman

I have already undressed; why should I get dressed again? I have washed my feet; why should I get them dirty again? My lover put his hand to the door, and I was thrilled that he was near. I was ready to let him come in. My hands were covered with myrrh, my fingers with liquid myrrh, as I grasped the handle of the door. I opened the door for my lover, but he had already gone. How I wanted to hear his voice! I looked for him, but couldn't find him; I called to him, but heard no answer.

Man to Woman – Song of Songs 6: 8–12

Let the king have sixty queens, eighty concubines, young women without number! But I love only one, and she is as lovely as a dove. She is her mother's only daughter, her mother's favourite child. All women look at her and praise her; queens and concubines sing her praises. Who is this whose glance is like the dawn? She is beautiful and bright, as dazzling as the sun or the moon. I have come down among the almond trees to see the young plants in the valley, to see the new leaves on the vines and the blossoms on the pomegranate trees. I am trembling; you have made me as eager for love as a chariot driver is for battle.

Man to Woman – Song of Songs 7: 1–9

What a magnificent young woman you are! How beautiful are your feet in sandals. The curve of your

thighs is like the work of an artist. A bowl is there, that never runs out of spiced wine. A sheaf of wheat is there, surrounded by lilies. Your breasts are like twin deer, like two gazelles. Your neck is like a tower of ivory. Your eyes are like the pools in the city of Heshbon, near the gate of that great city. Your nose is as lovely as the tower of Lebanon that stands guard at Damascus. Your head is held high like Mount Carmel. Your braided hair shines like the finest satin; its beauty could hold a king captive. How pretty you are, how beautiful; how complete the delights of your love. You are as graceful as a palm tree, and your breasts are clusters of dates. I will climb the palm tree and pick its fruit. To me your breasts are like bunches of grapes, your breath like the fragrance of apples, and your mouth like the finest wine.

Heady stuff! It must be repeated that some religious commentators "spiritualise" these words of Scripture and try to find hidden or esoteric meanings. It is always dangerous to spiritualise, to "find" hidden meanings in Scripture. God did not give us Scripture in order to hide its meaning from as many people as possible. Whilst much of its meaning can only be spiritually discerned through the inspiration of the Holy Spirit, that is not the same as saying that the words we are given are hidden, or the meanings twisted. What is preached is often foolishness to the world, especially in relation to the cross of Jesus (1 Corinthians 1: 18) but God in His wisdom made it impossible for people to know Him by means of their own wisdom (1 Corinthians 1: 21).

The reason for 'spiritualising' the Song of Songs seems most clearly to be to sever it from its obvious meaning – to translate it from the physical into the spiritual. This is Greek as opposed to Hebraic thinking (although we note that some Jewish commentators attempt the same thing in regards to The Song). But let us for just one moment assume that these interpreters are right and that the meaning of the Song is entirely spiritual. If this is the case, then what is the affirming imagery that God has chosen to get His point across to us? He might have chosen to liken His love as the pure love for a mother to her child. But instead, to emphasise this spiritual meaning He chose to liken it to the physical love between a man and a woman. Obviously, then, God is affirming such love and such physical anticipation as being altogether good and altogether wholesome. If it is good and wholesome then it is good for God's people as well.

The argument becomes circular. But the most obvious interpretation of the Song of Songs is exactly and precisely that it is a very earthy celebration of love between a man and a woman. We need then to note a few things about it:

Firstly, although the physical act of love-making is excitedly anticipated, it does not happen in the context of The Song. The lovers are waiting for each other – impatiently, to be sure – but they are waiting all the same. The message for readers is that we too are to wait until the time is right – and indeed not to let our feelings get the better of us.

Secondly, there is an imminency to the relationship. The lovers are not expected to wait for years and years for each other. Having declared their love in the most breathless way imaginable, they are looking forward to consummation of their relationship, to that true act of becoming *one flesh* in the fullest sense.

Thirdly, romantic love is affirmed, but it is not commanded! Not everyone will experience this same heady, extraordinary sense of longing. This is not the only pattern that can lead to a successful *one flesh* relationship. We mentioned in an earlier chapter that many marriages in biblical times were arranged marriages. It was entirely possible that the betrothed couple had only the slightest acquaintance. But, surprising as it may seem, even in the context of arranged marriages, in the Hebrew world there was an intention that there should be love and agreement of the 'to-be-betrothed'. This stands in stark contrast to the approach adopted to such 'arrangements' in many cultures, right up to the present day. We return to this later in this volume as we look at the sort of marriage rites with which the Lord Jesus would have been familiar, but it bears repetition: in the Judeo-Christian experience down through history, there has always been at least an expectation that the to-be-betrothed had the final say. They were not to be forced into marriage. This again would have been the Lord's expectation and clear understanding.

Fourthly, there was a clear expectation that this would be a monogamous relationship – the two would become *one* flesh. The man rejects any idea of having multiple wives, in spite of the fact that this was a practice in the ancient near east. The man declares that the King can have as many women as he wants (Song of Songs 6: 8), but this man desires just one! We note that king Solomon did have many wives and there is a school of thought that this series of poems were written by him (hence the alternative title Song of Solomon). But the Bible highlights that Solomon's taste for numerous women was a characteristic – indeed a profound weakness – that went on to destroy his dynasty. See 1 Kings 11: 1–11 for the sad summary. Solomon disobeyed God and his family would suffer the consequences. In spite of the fact that there are many characters in the Old Testament who had more than one wife, nowhere in the Scriptures is the practice affirmed. Wherever it occurs it leads to unhappiness, national or family weakness, and loss.

So, to summarise: love and romance, and physical love are affirmed in the Bible. Where the church, down through the ages, has got its witness to the world messed up in this important subject area, it is because it has applied Greek philosophical ideas rather than God's revealed Word as it tried clumsily to teach the world the virtues of love within a married state. The Song of Songs does indeed show us the potential joys of romantic love, but we are not "missing out" if this sort of heady love eludes us. There is not in fact first class and second class love. Expression of love is for the individuals and will be governed by many factors and circumstances – not least of which will be personal temperament. We have a sense that affirmed love amongst younger people is perfectly acceptable to God, there are no minimum age or minimum experience requirements that make us suitable lovers, beyond those set out by the law of the land. But, as we shall see later, some measure of emotional and physical maturity is essential to create stable relationships – and the joys of marriage.

"Happy are those who have been invited to the wedding feast"

4

BUILT TO LAST

Contract or Covenant?

If you have been following this book so far then you will have seen there is something very special that God has in mind for the humans He has placed into this world. People are made for relationship – first with God Himself and next with each other. Regarding relationships with each other, loneliness was the first enemy to be destroyed – God did this by creating us *from* ourselves. We are to be 'helpers' of each other, so making it possible to get through life sharing burdens and sharing joys. God has prepared something very special for us in terms of men and women – the possibility of a *one flesh* relationship which is designed to bring out the best in us, and to enable us to share with God in the creation process.

God certainly did not command a *one flesh* relationship for all people. After all, His own Son, Jesus, was never married. But in principle we can say that a *one flesh* relationship is God's pattern – for most of us. And why might this be? The answer is so that we can fulfil what we could call God's *prime directive* to humans, set out in Genesis 1: 28. "**Have many children, so that your**

descendents will live all over the earth and bring it under their control." A *one flesh* relationship is usually blessed with offspring as we humans share with God in the joy of the creative process – in other words we aim to have children. Again there will be some couples that do not want children, and others that cannot have children. But in general it can be said that children are part of God's intended blessing of the *one flesh* relationship that He has commanded.

When we speak of *one flesh* we are speaking in practical terms about marriage. The Judeo-Christian revelation from God is that a man shall leave and cleave, to use that wonderful old fashioned language. He will leave his parents and cleave to his wife (Genesis 2: 24). We find quite a bit about marriage in the Bible, as we would expect. Some of what we find is good, and some is bad – the Bible certainly provides examples for us to follow, and other examples to avoid like the plague! So what is marriage, precisely? Legal text books will give varying definitions of marriage, depending on the legal regime within which they are written. This in turn is dictated by the country concerned and the nature of its culture. Broadly, marriage is defined almost everywhere as the willing, life-long union of one man and one woman, in a type of 'contract' where each party acquires rights and obligations, to the exclusion of marriage or sexual relations with any other person. As there are differences between cultures and differing legal regimes, and as social *mores* change (for example marriage between groups of people is now being contemplated in some parts of the world) so the meaning of marriage becomes confused, blurred and devalued. For a seeker after God, the only definition of marriage to have any validity is that found in the Bible. And here we hit a slight problem....

The Bible does not give a single definition of marriage – in fact it gives no definition at all, so we have to discern the mind of God on this matter from what He has commanded about men and women through the laws He has given, and what the Scriptures teach us about male/female relationships in the lives of the real characters we come across in the Bible. As might be expected, there is a strong consistency between what God has commanded and what His Scriptures reveal. The biblical accounts we have of the lives of men and women do provide a very consistent idea of God's mind and will in these matters. There are as many negatives (accounts of tragic marriages and relationships) as there are positives (accounts of good marriages and relationships). Preparing this study, I originally listed the male/female relationships that we might usefully explore through the pages of Scripture, only to find there are just too many to look at in such a short book. Those I considered but left out are:

Abram and Sarai (or Abraham and Sarah)
Jacob and Rachel
Joseph and Potiphar's wife
Samson and Delilah
Hosea and Gomer
Mary and Joseph

Each of these accounts reveals aspects of God's attitude

to marriage and relationships and there are useful lessons to learn from them, lessons that we can definitely apply today. If any reader is really keen to look in much greater depth at the truths we can glean from the Bible about marriage, then I commend the book *Marriage and The Family* by A J Higgins MD (published by Gospel Tract Publications in 1988, ISBN 0948417293, but updated and expanded in recent years).

Allowing that the Bible does not in fact give a single unequivocal definition of marriage, we need to do a bit of work on this! We will start with a secular definition so as to see how far the secular world has shifted from the Scriptural position. The passage immediate below comes from a free online legal dictionary:

Marriage – the legal status, condition, or relationship that results from a contract by which one man and one woman, who have the capacity to enter into such an agreement, mutually promise to live together in the legal relationship of Husband and Wife for life, or until the legal termination of the relationship. Marriage is a legally sanctioned contract between a man and a woman. Entering into a marriage contract changes the legal status of both parties, giving husband and wife new rights and obligations. Public policy is strongly in favour of marriage based on the belief that it preserves the family unit. Traditionally, marriage has been viewed as vital to the preservation of morals and civilization.

The above is a definition that would probably be recognised in most Western countries, however from a Christian viewpoint it is both inadequate and misleading.

It speaks first of all of a "contract", which the Bible does not do. It speaks about the "legal termination" of the contract, which of course the Bible similarly does not, except in one tragic circumstance. But apart from those major flaws, the rest of the definition is unremarkable from a Christian viewpoint. So what can we say emphatically from a biblical Christian standpoint? Without getting too bogged down in detail and legalism, the following definition should be helpful:

A marriage is an unconditional, life long commitment of a man and a woman by which each take on certain rights and obligations regarding the other. This one flesh commitment assumes certain scriptural roles for each partner. Man and woman are complementary – they fulfil different roles, of which the clearest is procreation. The first task of marriage is to banish loneliness; the second is to enable man and woman to join with God in the process of creation.

Marriage between a man and a woman is not so much a contract, which has as its very nature a limited life and a defined end, but a covenant, which in biblical terms is always a life-long, or permanent, commitment. What is a covenant? Certainly in English law a covenant is seen as being somehow stronger and more binding than a mere contract. A covenant is usually made under seal, which adds to the solemnity of the agreement by affixing to the written instrument a "seal", which might be in hard wax or some other physical device. Such a document is shouting at us: *this is important*! – it is not just a day to day run-of-the-mill transaction. So a covenant is a special form of contract or agreement, often associated with agreements around transactions of very high value or of very high importance – something that people might well end up fighting over if the agreement is broken. In biblical terms a covenant is witnessed by others who are not a direct party to the agreement. We can readily see the analogy with marriage. The agreement is indeed a solemn one, no matter what feelings of romantic love may underpin it. The marriage ceremony is always witnessed by others. The seal on the marriage is traditionally the physical act of intimacy. Under English law even today the marriage contract is considered incomplete until the act of physical intimacy has first been encountered. Legally this is called "consummation" of the marriage, and an unconsummated marriage can be anulled.

We conclude this comparison of contract versus covenant from a biblical perspective – and now we can leave the lawyers behind! God is a covenant-keeping God. He strikes up covenants with mankind in various places in the Bible. Always God is the initiator and always He promises blessings to those who keep their side of the agreement. Bear in mind, of course, that such an agreement is never, in the Bible, between equals. God is almighty. We are but dust. The following ideas may be helpful as we consider the difference between a contract and a covenant, although in truth each idea is 'debatable':

* In a contract the services of people are in some way engaged; covenants engage the persons themselves.
* Contracts are made for a stated time period; covenants are forever.

* Contracts can be breached, with real loss to the contracting parties. Covenants cannot be broken, but if violated, then the violation results in personal loss, damaged future outlook and possibly in broken hearts.
* Contracts are witnessed by people with the Law as guarantor; covenants are witnessed by God with God as guarantor.

Why are we bothering with all this? Why is it necessary to analyse to the nth degree what a marriage is, and what it isn't? The answer quite simply is that without a measure of maturity in our thinking about relationships, our relationships will inevitably fall apart. If readers are so unconcerned about the future of their own relationships then now is the time to put down this book and turn on the telly. But if we believe in God (and perhaps even if we don't!) and believe that He wants us to have good relationships, then we have to invest some real effort. So let's stay with this a little longer – it will get easier later on, I promise!

Marriage as a Covenant.

In light of this understanding of a covenant as a permanent commitment, witnessed and guaranteed by God, we will shortly look once again at the three essential conditions of the marriage covenant that are pre-figured in Genesis 2:24: leaving, cleaving, and becoming one flesh.

The first description of marriage in the Bible shows us these three positive actions of leaving, cleaving and becoming one flesh (Gen 2: 24). This covenant pattern is established by God with the man and woman. Marriage as a covenant of companionship is expressed more explicitly later in Scripture in passages such as Malachi 2: 14: "**The Lord was witness to the *covenant* between you and the wife of your youth, to whom you have been faithless, though she is your *companion* and your wife by *covenant*"** (RSV – emphasis added). As a sacred covenant, human marriage in both Old and New Testaments is a type, or a symbol, through which God reveals His covenant relationship with His covenant people, the Hebrews in the Old Testament and the followers of Jesus (whether Jew or Gentile) in the New. (See also Proverbs 2: 17; Ezekiel 16: 8.)

Whilst marriage is seen biblically as a covenant entered into before God, and in satisfaction of God's command that two should become one, it is worth adding that in biblical times there were other expressions of this covenant relationship of marriage. Marriage was a covenant or an alliance between two families. So the two families became united, and by extending their kinship the overall size of the family group was increased. This was not insignificant in a society where responsibilities to relatives were accepted without question. The idea of covenant could also take on political overtones, as with the marriage between King Solomon and the Egyptian princess (1 Kings 11: 1), or Ahab of Israel to Jezebel of Tyre (1 Kings 16: 31). This idea of attempting to unite peoples through the marriage of their rulers continued to be a common practice right up to the nineteenth century –

British people remember how Queen Victoria engineered the marriages of her children widely to the royal families of Europe in the vain hope of tempering national rivalries.

Finally, the marriage covenant was analogous to the relationship that God had with the people Israel, which is an added argument for supposing that monogamy was the normal form of marriage. God expected His people to worship only Him – not the myriad of other "gods" that were available. The relationship of Christ to His church is also seen very clearly as that of Bridegroom to bride. See the lovely short book by Stephanie Cottam *Ready or Not – He Is Coming!* (Glory to Glory Publications 2012, ISBN 978-0-9567831-5-8) which looks at the return of Jesus for His church very much through the Hebrew marriage rites.

Leaving

The first dimension in establishing a marriage covenant is consciously to *leave* all other relationships, especially that closest relationship with father and mother: **"Therefore a man *leaves* his father and his mother"** (Gen 2: 24, emphasis added). This conscious leaving does not of course mean the abandonment of one's parents. The responsibility to "**Honour your father and mother**" (Exodus 20:12) is applied by Jesus to adults (Mark 7: 6–13). We cannot and should not evade our responsibility toward our parents as they grow old. Jesus scorned the hypocrisy of those who gave to the Temple the money they had set aside for their parents (Mark 7: 11–12). The

Bible nowhere suggests that married couples should sever their ties with their parents, but rather that they must "let go" of their former lives as sons and daughters in order to cement their relationships as husbands and wives.

"Leaving" is of course a strong word. It allows no room for going back. The ultimate purpose that God has for this oneness can never be known if there is not a conscious "leaving". Whilst this is addressed to the man in Genesis, this does not excuse the woman from its requirements. She also must leave, and in her case she leaves from being under her father's headship to being under headship in her husband's home. He leaves from the headship of his father's home to accept the God-given responsibility to become head of his own home. This in no way implies subjection of wife to husband (although historically this is often how God's command seems to have been worked out in practice). Too many men hide behind their wives' skirts here in the West and claim "equality" as a concept through which they think they can avoid their God-ordained responsibility to be head. When God seeks answers for the conduct of your family, men, He will not look to your wife for answers, He will look first and foremost to you! That's a tough requirement which is not often preached in today's emptying churches. But whether faithfully preached or not, whether you acknowledge it or not, man, God will first address you for answers.

Once again the author senses hackles rising and both men and women angrily rejecting God's ordinance – His plan. And once again you are urged at this stage to "park" your difficulties whilst our biblical exploration plays out.

If you really want to have a lasting *one flesh* relationship, then the only way to guarantee you will set out on the right path is to learn from the Maker's Instructions. Some will immediately complain, "What happens if the father is hateful, abusive, lazy, absent – or someone who actively rejects Jesus?" All these seem to be real impediments to founding a household and a home where the husband sets the moral tone. Readers may say that Mr Sammons simply does not know what he is talking about, or that he is gratuitously interpreting Scripture in the man's favour whilst ignoring the real-world situations that so often make this biblical ideal completely impossible to live out in practice. I would offer only this thought in reply: my own father rejected Jesus (he was what is called an atheist – someone who denies the existence of God) and in no way sought to set the moral or spiritual tone of his household. In that sense he was an "absentee father". The author's mother in fact was forced to act as true spiritual head of the household because of her husband's spiritual blindness and antipathy. God both makes allowances for such situations and provides the necessary anointing for another to be *de facto* head where this is necessary. But it is not His plan, and the man is *never* released from his primary obligation before God.

What "leaving" means is that all lesser relationships must give way to the newly formed marital relationship. A conscious leaving must occur in order to cement the covenant relationship of husband and wife. This principle of leaving applies in the same way to our covenant relationship with God. We remind ourselves that the disciples "*left* **everything and followed Him**" (Luke 5:11). Physically leaving may not be a problem, indeed many will already have left home for tertiary education or career reasons. But mentally leaving may indeed be a problem! Think of it in these terms for a moment: it is often hard for a baby to leave the security and familiarity of the mother's womb. It may seem cruel for a midwife to cut the umbilical cord that binds baby to mother. But it is absolutely essential for the growth and development of the baby. It can be hard for children to leave their parents – and even harder for parents to let their children go, for example, to a school that is away from home. In the same way that babies cannot grow unless they leave their mother's womb and children cannot obtain their education unless they go to school, so a marriage cannot develop and mature unless both man and woman are willing to leave their parents in order to cement their new *one flesh* relationship, becoming a new family.

Cleaving

The second key aspect of the marriage covenant is *cleaving*: "**Therefore a man leaves his father and his mother and *cleaves* to his wife, and they become one flesh**" (Genesis 2: 24, RSV, emphasis added). A man and a woman must leave all lesser relationships in order to cleave, that is, to cement their new relationship and establish a new home. The Hebrew word for "cleave" suggests the idea of being permanently joined together, or in modern terms, the analogy would be being glued together. It is one of the words frequently used to express the covenant commitment of the people to God: "**You shall fear the L**ORD **your God; you shall serve him and** *cleave* **to him, and by his name you shall swear**" (RSV Deuteronomy 10: 20, emphasis added; cf. 11: 22; 13: 4; 30: 20). The same Hebrew word is used to describe Ruth's single-minded refusal to leave her mother-in-law Naomi. The old Authorised Version renders this "**Ruth clave unto her**" (Ruth 1: 14, AV).

In the sight of God, cleaving means wholehearted commitment which spills over to every area of our being. It involves complete loyalty to your *one flesh* partner. We note that in cleaving to his wife this excludes marital unfaithfulness. A man cannot be glued to his wife and flirt or engage in sexual intercourse with another woman. The two are mutually exclusive.

In the marriage covenant, cleaving allows no "freedom" to leave when the relationship is no longer satisfying. If there is in the minds of prospective partners any idea of a "freedom to leave" as a real option, this negates completely the effort to develop a relationship characterized by covenant faithfulness. Irrespective of what modern lawyers tell us, the idea of a pre-nuptial agreement relating to divorce actually destroys any pretence of marriage as the *one flesh* relationship ordained by God. We could go as far as saying that in the presence of a pre-nuptial agreement, the parties have emphatically denied that they are married in anything other than a convenient manner – indeed such a 'marriage' could be described as a marriage of convenience! If there is a conscious plan for circumstances where the covenant is to be broken, then the covenant does not in fact exist. We might add, if there is a plan to keep divorce as a sort of escape clause to the marriage agreement, then this indicates a flaw in the relationship, no matter how tiny that flaw may be. The many forces in society working to destroy marriages will have little difficulty opening up that flaw.

When considering marriage we should ask ourselves: *am I willing to make a lifetime commitment to my prospective spouse*, and, in the terms of the traditional Church of England marriage rite to make this commitment "for better or for worse till death do us part"? And once we are married, cleaving means continually asking ourselves: *will this attitude, or word, or action or decision draw us closer together as a couple or drive us further apart*? Will it build and affirm or undermine our relationship? Certainly it must be said that for a Christian committed to living by the principles set out in God's Word, any action that weakens this *cleaving* has to be considered as running counter to God's purpose for the marriage covenant.

Becoming One Flesh

The third dimension of the marriage covenant is that they **"become *one flesh"*** (Gen 2:24, RSV). We note the progression; leaving, then cleaving, then becoming one flesh. As husband and wife leave lesser relationships, so they learn to cling to or cleave to one another. So in a way that it is difficult for us to define fully, they become a new entity, "one flesh." As we have said before, 1+1=1.

It is to be hoped by now in our discussions over these first four chapters we have recognised that *one flesh* means more than just the aspect of physical intimacy. The phrase is all too often assumed to refer primarily to sexual union. To become "one flesh" (Gen 2: 24) means *to become a single functioning unit* that draws its strength from itself. Being one flesh entails the complete identification of one personality with the other in a community of interests and pursuits, a union that is consummated in the act of physical intimacy. We noted earlier in this book that it is an observable fact that couples who have been married for a long time do increasingly think, act and feel as one. They enjoy the same humour, can understand each other's thoughts from a flash in the eyes, have a physical intimacy that is theirs alone. This is why divorce is an unmitigated personal disaster. Even where divorce seems to address or to "put right" serious problems, ungluing and tearing apart that which has been once joined inevitably leaves fractures. In mechanical terms, fractures lead to permanent weakness. Is it too much of a leap to say that the same is true of *one flesh* relationships torn apart – that they also leave permanent fractures?

For completeness and accuracy we need to add that the term "one flesh" in the Bible *does* also refer to the physical or sexual aspect of marriage. Paul explicitly uses the term in this way when he refers to sexual union between a man and a harlot (1 Corinthians 6:16). Sexual intercourse as a physical act does not automatically assure that a man and a woman become *one* as an emotional and spiritual unity. What it does do is to mimic, or it masquerades as, the act of consummating a one flesh relationship that does not exist – and often where there is no intention of creating one. Sexual intercourse without the intention of a *one flesh* spiritual communion all too often leaves men and women divided, alienated, and bitter toward each other. Sexual intercourse itself does not bring about *real* oneness.

If readers have questions and difficulties with this, then hopefully they will be addressed adequately later in this study. What we are considering from a biblical standpoint is extraordinarily challenging to our modern world and to the various cultures and sub-cultures within it. But we can summarise: to achieve the *one flesh* unity that is God's plan and intention, sexual intercourse within marriage is and must be a natural fruit of love. To share our bodies is a physical expression of the sharing of our minds and ambitions, of hopes and fears, our very selves. If it is not the expression of genuine love and genuine respect, and full commitment, then it offers only a transient physical contact while the partners remain mentally and spiritually apart.

It all Takes Time....

A man and a woman who go through a marriage ceremony do not automatically become "one flesh" as they exchange their marriage vows. Legally, the limitations of the vows, or the incompleteness of the vows alone, has always been recognised by the legal requirement to consummate the marriage – from a legal standpoint this at very minimum demonstrates the unequivocal intention of the partners to be a *one flesh* unity. What they have said with their mouths they have confirmed with their bodies.

Is there a loss of independence in this coming together? Are we becoming robotised as God's "goody goody two-shoes"? Surely we should enjoy ourselves as we see fit? Once again the rubber really hits the road on this question. Humans continuously want to go their own way as regards God's holy plans, as regards His holy design and intention. That's what the account in Genesis chapter 3 teaches us. We hate the idea of obedience to God and want to be 'god' over our own lives. We think we have a "right" to independence and autonomy – and indeed much in our culture teaches us that this is precisely so. This is why "human rights" lawyers are doing rather nicely today - in the Western world, at any rate! At kindergarten, children learn about their "rights" from the youngest possible age, so it is unsurprising that our post-Christian culture pits us more and more directly against biblical standards. Within marriage the personalities of the man and woman remain free. God expects us and wants us to become more complete in ourselves and in Him. It might be added that any curtailment of our autonomy is for our own good! But we scream back angrily – "I will decide what's good for me!" It is a hollow cry because God has wisely set limits on our self expression, and ultimately we must answer to Him for the way we conduct our lives.

So in marriage our personalities will and should remain free and independent. But man and woman continue "naturally" to want to assert their respective wills, and this can be destructive. As a couple live together as husband and wife, they discover that they must preserve their individuality while striving to become one. This is a learning process. Rome was not built in a day, and nor is a marriage. We need to be alert to the fact that our differences can be a point of tension between us. We should not allow our differences to divide us but instead must learn to accept our differences and see them not so much as *in opposition* but rather as *complementary*. Husband and wife can still be themselves and yet come into unity. The husband must learn to accept his wife as she is *because he needs to be accepted as he is*. Our differences can contribute to achieving our *one flesh* oneness when they are accepted as being complementary and not contradictory.

Build to last is the corporate ethos, if not literally the advertising slogan, of any builder who takes pride in his work. It takes time to build a marriage, and, in common with the good builder, we may have to sweat and worry, to plan and do much "heavy lifting" to build the marriage that will last. Whilst the gift of children is not for all married couples, we can recognise God's brilliant master plan for the one flesh relationship quite literally in the faces of children. Children display some of the unique features of both mother and father. When they are born, we see something amazing and marvellous – and permanent. Parents can see something of each other in the new baby, and are reminded that each cell of that new person reflects something of each of them. The father cannot take away his features, nor the mother her features, from their children! The child is now the living entity who represents the parents' one flesh relationship. In their children, husband and wife are indissolubly united into one person. The child is in a very real sense the output of that built-to-last relationship.

What happens biologically in children can be said to happen psychologically in the husband/wife one flesh relationship as the two gradually become one – a new functioning unity. Becoming "one flesh" also implies continuity. We cannot become one flesh with a succession of husbands and wives. This is why the modern practice which we might describe as *serial monogamy* must be rejected as impractical (it does not work) and injurious (it damages us). The fractures occasioned by a previous broken married relationship become weaknesses that are carried into the next – whether the couples bother to marry or not. This sad reality seems to be borne out by statistics – second marriages after divorce are even more frangible than first marriages.

Repeat marriages, of course, attempt to defeat the biblical plan for marriage which is to develop a *permanent one flesh* relationship. It is perhaps superfluous to add that the *one flesh* principle excludes polygamy and extra-marital relationships of all kinds, because no man can become "one flesh" with more than one woman. Those we learn about in the Old Testament who violated the "one flesh" principle by taking more than one wife always paid a heavy price for their transgressions. We see problems of all sorts played out, particularly as wives became jealous or felt exploited, degraded, or hated.

It may that, at the end of this chapter some readers will be feeling that God's demands are just too hard, that they must be impossible to live out in practice. If you are feeling depressed or frightened at this stage, then I would simply say "stay with it"! There *is* good news! What God has set out before us as His pattern for love relationships is not impossible – and indeed the existence of many good and happy marriages surely demonstrates that this is the case. And always remember this; the God who loves each one of us sufficiently to give His own Son to carry the punishment that should have been ours, to die in our place, can surely be trusted in this intimate matter of founding a good and wholesome marriage.

*"Happy are those who have been invited
to the wedding feast"*

5

TRUE ROMANCE —
RUTH AND BOAZ

The most unpopular virtue

We ended the last chapter on a bit of a low note, by confronting the reality that God's pattern for love relationships is almost well nigh impossible to attain. Perhaps we should immediately qualify that by saying that God's pattern for love relationships is almost well nigh impossible to attain *by our own human efforts unaided*. Like the disciples (in Matthew 19: 10) we might well conclude at this stage: "**If this is how it is between a man and his wife, it is better not to marry**." Although the disciples were then speaking specifically about divorce, their sentiment might easily have been applied by them to the whole area of marriage, because marriage – as God intends it – makes many high-principled demands upon us. Are we up to it? Can we *ever* be up to it?

The good news is that we can. C S Lewis (actual name Clive Staples Lewis, died November 1963 but universally known simply as CS Lewis), the novelist and poet best known for *The Chronicles of Narnia* and his Christian apologetic, *The Problem of Pain*, wrote a very helpful book called *Mere Christianity* which is still widely read. In Part 3 of the book, "Christian Morality", he allocates a short chapter to *Sexual Morality* and another to *Christian Marriage*. In these two chapters, in Lewis' inimitable and quite humorous style, he makes the simple case that whilst sexual appetite is a good thing and a gift from God, it has been perverted by our human natures into something unrecognisable for its intended purpose. In the chapter on marriage Lewis makes the valid and obvious point that we need to ask for God's help to live out the ethic that God requires. But he also comments that God understands our fallen nature and that God makes allowances where we fall. I will not steal CS Lewis' thunder by quoting him or following his argument in detail, except in the paragraph immediately below. As *Mere Christianity* is a classic, I would suggest that truly interested readers should make an effort to get a copy and enjoy it fully.

CS Lewis makes the point that "chastity" is the most unpopular of the Christian virtues. In this he is surely correct. The Christian rule is either marriage, with complete faithfulness to your spouse, or else total abstinence. As Lewis says, this is so difficult and so contrary to our human instincts that either Christianity is wrong or our sexual instinct *as it now is* has gone wrong. Lewis affirms that he believes that it is the instinct that has gone wrong. We can see this straightforwardly, says Lewis. The biological purpose of sex is children, in the same way that the biological purpose of food is to keep the body running properly. If we eat whenever we are inclined, we will probably eat too much, but not terrifically too much. A man might eat enough for two, but he will not eat enough for ten. The appetite goes a little beyond its biological purpose, but not enormously. But if a healthy young man indulged his sexual appetite whenever he felt inclined, and if each act produced a baby, then in ten years he might easily populate a small village. "This appetite" says Lewis "is in ludicrous and preposterous excess of its function".

In the same way, says Lewis, a theatre can usually get a large audience for a striptease show. But what if you went to a country where you could get a large audience to a theatre simply by bringing a covered plate on to a stage and then slowly lifting the cover to let everyone see that it contained a mutton chop or a piece of bacon? You would think that something had gone wrong in that country with people's appetite for food – either that or you would conclude perhaps that the people were starving. Does the striptease act result from sexual starvation or from sexual corruption? If we believed that sexual starvation was the culprit, we would need to find the evidence. As we look at our modern world (sadly even more corrupted than when Lewis was writing in the 1950s), we see not sexual starvation, but a society totally absorbed in sexual licence. More and more licence has not brought happiness or contentment, rather the reverse.

So, if we want to live by godly standards, we are up against a powerful alliance of enemies: our own natural inclinations, the propaganda of the world, and the propaganda of the devil – the old liar we met in Chapter 3. Or as people used to say, we are up against *the world, the flesh and the devil*. All this is helpful to know, but how do we get beyond head knowledge to heart engagement? From knowing what is wrong to wanting to do what's right? We will look again, later in this book, at the various enemies we encounter as ordinary people who would like to live out a *one flesh* relationship if only we thought it were possible. But for the remainder of this chapter, we are going to look at a second love story in the Old Testament to demonstrate once again that God very much approves of that emotion we call romantic love, and has a purpose for it. Moreover, we reflect on the fact that, in God's economy, romantic love can both bless us and bring glory to His Name.

Man Meets Woman

The peaceful story of Ruth is set in the violent times of the book of Judges. To escape famine in the land of Judah (part of modern Israel) Elimelech, his wife Naomi and two sons, Mahlon and Chilion, move east and across the river Jordan to Moab where they settle. Some time later Elimelech died. The two sons, after marrying Moabite women, also died, leaving Naomi as a widow with two daughters-in-law. The famine in Judah having ended, Naomi determines to return home but urges her daughters-in-law to remain among their own kinsfolk. Of the two, it is Ruth who determines to stay with Naomi, come what may. The Hebrew word that is used in the Old Testament is that Ruth *cleaved* to (or clung to) Naomi. It is a strong word and the same verb as used in Genesis 2: 24 for cleaving in marriage.

Now dear reader, you have a choice! You can get yourself a Bible and read the whole of the story of Ruth and Boaz (which I recommend!) or you can allow me to summarise it for you, but I will rather spoil the story by telling you the end before you have had a chance to enjoy the whole rather romantic story from the beginning. Which Bible translation you use is pretty much immaterial, but in this book we continue to use the Good News translation, which is a paraphrase. The choice is yours! If you decide to read the book of Ruth then you may want to pause here before going further. It should be stated straight away that the real purpose of the Book of Ruth is *not* to give us a beautiful love story. The key purpose of the book of Ruth is authentication of the Davidic line on the throne of Israel – because Ruth was the great grandmother of King David. The book's major theme is redemption, a word that occurs 23 times in the text. Boaz acts as a redeemer by buying back Naomi's land, marrying Ruth and fathering a son to keep the family line alive. This role of "Kinsman – Redeemer" is symbolic of the redeeming work of Jesus upon the cross. The real purpose of the Book of Ruth is the promise of Jesus. However this is way beyond the scope of our study, which we will restrict to the *man meets woman* dimension of the story.

Mother-in-law Naomi has decided to return to Judah

(in Israel) and told her two daughters-in-law to return to their own relatives and build a new life for themselves. We pick up the story at Ruth 1: 16

But Ruth answered, "Don't ask me to leave you! Let me go with you. Wherever you go, I will go; wherever you live, I will live. Your people will be my people, and your God will be my God. Wherever you die, I will die, and that is where I will be buried. May the Lord's worst punishment come upon me if I let anything but death separate me from you!"

As we noted elsewhere, the actual word used in verse 14 says that Ruth clung to Naomi (or in the really old fashioned English translations, she "clave" to Naomi). Ruth has demonstrated the seriousness of her intention to remain by making five clear commitments (vv. 16 and 17). We inevitably contrast Ruth's response to Naomi's encouragement to return to their own Moabite "gods" (1: 15). Ruth decides to follow the God of Israel and His laws. Ruth's appeal to Naomi's God decides the matter – they will return to Israel together. Their arrival in Bethlehem is traumatic for Naomi. Having left Bethlehem with a husband and two sons, she returns empty and asks to be called "Bitter" (v. 20). Some time later Ruth asks Naomi's permission to do the only "work" that destitute women were able to do, that was to freely gather the left-overs during the harvest, actually following the harvesters to pick up what they discarded. This was as close to social security as this iron-age society provided and shows how hard life had become for the two women. Naomi had a rich and influential relative, Boaz, who was a relative of Elimelech. We pick up the story in Ruth 2: 3.

Ruth went out to the fields and walked behind the workers, picking up the heads of grain which they left. It so happened that she was in a field that belonged to Boaz. Some time later Boaz himself arrived from Bethlehem and greeted the workers. "The Lord be with you!" he said.

"The Lord bless you!" they answered.

Boaz asked the man in charge, "Who is that young woman?"

The man answered, "She is the foreigner who came back from Moab with Naomi. She asked me to let her follow the workers and gather grain. She has been working since early morning and has just now stopped to rest for a while under the shelter."

Then Boaz said to Ruth, "Let me give you some advice. Don't gather grain anywhere except in this field. Work with the women here; watch them to see where they are reaping and stay with them. I have ordered my men not to molest you. And whenever you are thirsty, go and drink from the water jars that they have filled."

Ruth bowed down with her face touching the ground, and said to Boaz, "Why should you be so concerned about me? Why should you be so kind to a foreigner?"

Boaz answered, "I have heard about everything

that you have done for your mother-in-law since your husband died. I know how you left your father and mother and your own country and how you came to live among a people you had never known before. May the Lord reward you for what you have done. May you have a full reward from the Lord God of Israel, to whom you have come for protection!"

Ruth answered, "You are very kind to me, sir. You have made me feel better by speaking gently to me, even though I am not the equal of one of your servants."

At mealtime Boaz said to Ruth, "Come and have a piece of bread, and dip it in the sauce." So she sat with the workers, and Boaz passed some roasted grain to her. She ate until she was satisfied, and she still had some food left over. After she had left to go and gather grain, Boaz ordered the workers, "Let her gather grain even where the bundles are lying, and don't say anything to stop her. Besides that, pull out some heads of grain from the bundles and leave them for her to pick up." So Ruth gathered grain in the field until evening, and when she had beaten it out, she found she had nearly twenty-five pounds.

She took the grain back into town and showed her mother-in-law how much she had gathered. She also gave her the food left over from the meal. Naomi asked her, "Where did you gather all this grain today? Whose field have you been working in? May God bless the man who took an interest in you!" So Ruth told Naomi that she had been working in a field belonging to a man named Boaz. "May the Lord bless Boaz!" Naomi exclaimed. "The Lord always keeps his promises to the living and the dead." And she went on, "That man is a close relative of ours, one of those responsible for taking care of us."

Then Ruth said, "Best of all, he told me to keep gathering grain with his workers until they finish the harvest."

Naomi said to Ruth, "Yes, daughter, it will be better for you to work with the women in Boaz' field. You might be molested if you went to someone else's field." So Ruth worked with them and gathered grain until all the barley and wheat had been harvested. And she continued to live with her mother-in-law.

We can probably see where this story is taking us by now. The author was once at a Bible study and one of the women attending said at this point, "Obviously Boaz fancied Ruth!" We might think that this is to somewhat over-simplify what is happening here! As a wealthy land owner, we may assume Boaz was somewhat older than Ruth and possibly he was looking for a wife. But the last place he would look, especially in Israel, was for a Moabite bride, because the Israelites had had a chequered history with and against the Moabites. But Boaz had noted good things about Ruth (vv. 11–12) and it was these things, it seems, that first aroused his interest in her. At this point his interest seems to have limited itself to giving her protection and a slightly easier opportunity to "glean" corn. His principal motive for doing this might well have been to bless Naomi, who was a relative and to whom he owed a responsibility. But if he had been thinking in terms of a wife, he certainly would have had good down-to-earth advice about looking for the things that really matter, as we see in the book of Proverbs. This book may have been roughly contemporary with the time of Ruth, but the collected wisdom of Proverbs may have been in circulation as a sort of folk-ethic hundreds of years earlier. So what does a sensible man look for in a good wife?

Proverbs 31: 10–31

How hard it is to find a capable wife! She is worth far more than jewels! Her husband puts his confidence in her, and he will never be poor. As long as she lives, she does him good and never harm. She keeps herself busy making wool and linen cloth. She brings home food from out-of-the-way places, as merchant ships do. She gets up before daylight to prepare food for her family and to tell her servant women what to do. She looks at land and buys it, and with money she has earned she plants a vineyard. She is a hard worker, strong and industrious. She knows the value of everything she makes, and works late into the night. She spins her own thread and weaves her own cloth. She is generous to the poor and needy. She doesn't worry when it snows, because her family has warm clothing. She makes bedspreads and wears clothes of fine purple linen. Her husband is well known, one of the leading citizens. She makes clothes and belts, and sells them to

merchants. She is strong and respected and not afraid of the future. She speaks with a gentle wisdom. She is always busy and looks after her family's needs. Her children show their appreciation, and her husband praises her. He says, "Many women are good wives, but you are the best of them all." Charm is deceptive and beauty disappears, but a woman who honours the Lord should be praised. Give her credit for all she does. She deserves the respect of everyone.

Ruth "ticked all the right boxes" at verses 14, 15, 27 and 30. Boaz credited Ruth as he ought to (verse 31). The fact that Ruth ticked at least four "boxes" suggests that she would be likely to tick all the others as well! Boaz may have "twigged" this straightaway. Ruth could be quite a catch for a man looking for a good and dependable wife! But it is Naomi who puts two and two together to make exactly the right number (see 3: 1)! She senses, perhaps, that Boaz's interest might be more than just charity. Naomi's advice sounds like scheming – but we might think, well why not? Boaz needed a wife and Naomi knew the qualities of this wonderfully loyal and loving girl. Could there be a match in the making? In a sense Naomi acts as the introducer in a way analogous to God introducing Eve to Adam, and the loyal servant introducing Rebecca to Isaac. So what is Naomi's scheme? It is Naomi speaking, and we pick up the story at Ruth 3: 2.

Remember that this man Boaz, whose women you have been working with, is our relative. Now listen. This evening he will be threshing the barley. So wash yourself, put on some perfume, and get dressed in your best clothes. Then go where he is threshing, but don't let him know you are there until he has finished eating and drinking. Be sure to notice where he lies down, and after he falls asleep, go and lift the covers and lie down at his feet. He will tell you what to do."

Ruth answered, "I will do everything you say." So Ruth went to the threshing place and did just what her mother-in-law had told her. When Boaz had finished eating and drinking, he was in a good mood. He went to the pile of barley and lay down to sleep. Ruth slipped over quietly, lifted the covers and lay down at his feet.

During the night he woke up suddenly, turned over, and was surprised to find a woman lying at his feet. "Who are you?" he asked.

"It's Ruth, sir," she answered. "Because you are a close relative, you are responsible for taking care of me. So please marry me."

"The Lord bless you," he said. "You are showing even greater family loyalty in what you are doing now than in what you did for your mother-in-law. You might have gone looking for a young man, either rich or poor, but you haven't. Now don't worry, Ruth. I will do everything you ask; as everyone in town knows, you are a fine woman. It is true that I am a close relative and am responsible for you, but there is a man who is a closer relative than I am. Stay here

the rest of the night, and in the morning we will find out whether or not he will take responsibility for you. If so, well and good; if not, then I swear by the living Lord that I will take the responsibility. Now lie down and stay here till morning." So she lay there at his feet, but she got up before it was light enough for her to be seen, because Boaz did not want anyone to know that she had been there.

Naomi's plan may sound slightly odd until we understand that Naomi believed that Boaz was her nearest kinsman, giving him the right of first refusal to marry into the family of his dead relative, where it was necessary to preserve the family line. According to Israelite law (Deuteronomy 25: 5ff) it was the duty of Boaz to marry Ruth to raise up "seed to the dead" – in this case it was Ruth's deceased husband (which we assume was Chilion, although the Bible does not specifically say so) who had died without children, which in turn gave rise to the general responsibility of the closest male relative to marry the widow.

Boaz's response to Ruth is gentlemanly in the extreme. He explains the situation that he is *not* the nearest kinsman, but promises to take care of the necessary procedures the very next day. The next day Boaz sought out the closer relative and before witnesses asked him to declare his hand. Would he buy-in to Naomi's property and would he marry Ruth? The closer relative wants the land but declines the wife and so loses his option (Ruth Chapter 4).

All this might sound alien to our way of thinking, but reflects the religious and legal norms of ancient Israel. Boaz, having found the field clear, as it were, now has first refusal, and he accepts the hand of the lovely Ruth. We repeat that the story of Ruth is significant at a number of levels and is not primarily about marriage – nor romance. But it still shows how intimately concerned God is with such matters that He has set out laws about what should happen in tragic circumstances where family lines are cut off through untimely death. But also and more generally, that God will "arrange" things so that His people can find good mates.

Bringing it right up to date....

Having looked at an undeniably romantic story dating back some three thousand years, what do we learn that is of relevance today? Leaving aside the primary purpose of the Book of Ruth – to confirm the authenticity of King David's genealogy (which is vital as it speaks to us of the genealogy of Jesus) – what are we left with? Naomi's and Ruth's practical needs were best met by marriage, and it seems that God directly provided for that need in the shape of the extremely eligible bachelor, Boaz. God meets our needs, especially when we allow Him to do so, and doubly so as we honour Him with our lives. The wise and lovely Ruth honoured Naomi's God, the one true God, by giving up her ancestral "gods" and placing herself at His mercy. (Ruth 1: 16). That there were feelings stirring between Boaz and Ruth, for whom Boaz had become very much a white knight, rescuing her (and Naomi) from their economic and social plight, scarcely seems necessary to say. But Boaz was also an honourable man, pledging himself to look after a woman whose position without him would be precarious. Boaz provided a home, social status and protection to someone who might without that loving support have been very much an outcast. In these terms our minds naturally think of Joseph, who stood by Mary the mother of Jesus and provided for her a home and social status, protection and a family name for Jesus, for he too was an honourable man.

The Bible shows us that a concerned God cares and will intervene. In their different ways, Naomi, Ruth and Boaz all co-operated with God in His grand design. And they were blessed for doing so. Christians do not lightly think of their God as *Jehovah Jireh* – the Lord Who Provides (Genesis 22: 14). This is the experience of His faithful people down three millennia and more. He provides good things to those who place their trust in Him, and for all mankind He provided His Son, as an atoning sacrifice for our sins. So Christians are glad enough to trust their God who provides good things – including, as necessary, husbands and wives. But what do modern men and women place their trust in, as they look for a possible mate?

Plato considered love to be a serious mental disease. Aristotle thought of it as a single soul inhabiting two bodies. People who lived through the 1980s may well remember Tina Turner's hit song, *What's Love Got to Do With It?* with its memorable and catchy refrain "What's love but a second-hand emotion?" Two months before this book was written two serious books were published in the English language as meditations on 'love'. The first was "In Praise of Love" by French philosopher Alain Badiou/Nicolas Truong. Badiou considered that there are three prevailing views of 'love'. Love can be an illusion, to be treated with scepticism; it can be a transactional and unsentimental contract; and it can be a truly ecstatic encounter between two individuals. But Mr Badiou was inclined to reject all three prevailing ideas in favour of his own, which is that love is the decision to live life through two perspectives, that between the lover and the beloved. Love, he went on to comment, is "a construction" and "a life that is being made, no longer from the perspectives of One, but from the perspective of Two."

We are used to the idea of France being the most secular State in Europe (bar Belgium, which some experts say is even more hostile to organised religion) so it is perhaps unsurprising that a French philosopher (and the French do love their philosophers!) by thinking his way through the subject, should reach a construct that is almost diametrically opposed to the revelation of the Bible. In contrast to Badiou's construct, a Christian would say that love is a life where two sets of interests and two personalities become ever more closely entwined, as the two people discover and live out the reality of 1+1=1, as two become *one flesh*. In one area, however, we might agree with Badiou. He sees risk as central to love. In the English language we have an old saying that, "It is better to have loved and lost, than never to have loved at all." No doubt most people would recognise this and probably agree with the sentiment. There is a risk in trying to form a relationship of complementaries, of X and Y chromosomes. The old bard William Shakespeare in his *A Midsummer Night's Dream* wrote "The course of true love never did run smooth." Again there will be many who can identify with that statement. There are all too often "problems" with love – but maybe that is because we try to set up our loving relationships without reference to God and to His plans for our lives. We prefer too much our own agendas.

Badiou notes that a loving relationship demands multiple and shared perspectives. This is where risk comes in, as there will always be tensions and incongruencies between a couple. Badiou sees that people all too often try to find a "risk free option" in relationships, for example by using internet dating sites, sharing photos, and details of horoscope signs, dates of birth, details of personal tastes and so on to "match-up" the optimum partner. But, says Badiou, this is to try to avoid the very essence of love, which must involve the presence of risk, the need for vulnerability and the possibility of failure.

The second book was entitled *The Science of Love and Betrayal* by Robin Dunbar, a professor of evolutionary anthropology. Some might dismiss his book similarly as being very one-sided, based as it must be on one of the theories of evolution (or *the religion of evolution* as some people now call it). Dunbar seeks to link humans' romantic behaviour to psychological, social, 'evolutionary' and historical contexts that Dunbar believes have helped to shape it. Dunbar is fascinated that humans should have a preference for pair-bonding when, he notes, this monogamy is disadvantageous in terms of "evolution". Dunbar notes that monogamy is not peculiar to humans, but that what is unique is the intensity of the feelings, with every human culture in history displaying this same complex sense of longing for a mate. Dunbar speculates that "love" feelings go through the heady intensity of the "falling" stage, through stubborn persistence in family affections, through to the bitterness of betrayal.

On the latter point, of male-female love being common to all cultures and historic ages, we can happily agree with Mr Dunbar. But it is interesting (and amusing) that an *evolutionary specialist* such as Mr Dunbar, who puzzles that humans routinely break the evolutionists' pet theory which should lead us towards polygamous behaviour, should miss the most obvious explanation for our behaviour – the one set out in Genesis chapter 2. We were *designed* for one another, designed for a one flesh expression of love and personality. And the bitterness of betrayal on which Mr Dunbar reflects can surely best be explained in terms of not tearing apart what God has joined together, because it is just too painful.

"Happy are those who have been invited to the wedding feast"

6

THE MARRIAGE THAT ISN'T....

Marriage Lite

Whilst this book is sub-titled ***What Jesus Taught About Love, Relationships, Marriage and a Lot More***, up to this point we have not actually studied much about what Jesus actually said. We have spent time looking at what the Bible of His day (what we call the "Old Testament") says about *two becoming one*, and we have seen that Jesus affirmed that. Having affirmed the rightness of Scripture on this important and foundational subject, Jesus' teaching was more directed towards practicalities. So for the remainder of this book we also will focus on practicalities, but with a keen eye to what the Lord Jesus said.

If we have gleaned nothing else in this book so far, we have understood that there is something very special and very precious, about the *one flesh* relationship for which we were designed. And that however counter-cultural it may be, the one flesh relationship is to be enjoyed with *one person*. That is part of the Maker's design and it is set out in The Maker's Instructions, as we saw in Chapter 1.

If there is a single social change in the Western world over the past 100 years that has become almost universal, it is the belief that the *status* of marriage is relatively unimportant and that, instead, it is the *quality* of the relationship that is all-important. Because of the rising divorce rate there is an in-built assumption that *people have chosen the wrong partner* and that the answer to this problem is to *be more sure of who the right partner is*. And the way to achieve that is for couples to live together as a sort of trial marriage. Whether the rising divorce rate was actually linked in some way to the rising rate of cohabitation was a subject rarely discussed in the "swinging sixties" when society finally abandoned its embarrassment about cohabitation, and when cohabitation started to become the norm amongst the intelligentsia.

In January 1994 the BBC launched its Year of The Family with a programme called "The Family Show". Its presenter, Nick Ross, asked "childcare expert" Penelope Leach about the prospects for children born outside of marriage. Her reply was illuminating:

> You said born outside marriage. What's that got to do with anything? There are no statistics whatsoever that suggest marriage – that piece of paper – makes any difference at all. What matters is relationships.

Leach's view was and remains extremely popular amongst social policy intellectuals. Whilst it had become obvious in the 1990s that being brought up by a single parent brought a range of disadvantages to the child, the politically correct "inclusive" response was to say that marriage was not to be promoted, but rather that the quality of good relationships was to be promoted, with the status of marriage being an irrelevance. That became the stated position of the UK Labour party in the 1990s, when the then Home Secretary Jack Straw famously said, "We shouldn't get in a paddy about the decline of marriage", and went on, "other kinds of families, including single-parent families, parents who live together without choosing to marry, and step-families, can do just as well for their children" (*Daily Mail,* 16 June, 1999). What was a stated view on the Left in the 1990s is broadly the *de facto* view of all the political parties in the second decade of the twenty-first century.

So why not cohabit? If people love each other then what is wrong with entering into a full adult relationship? If a couple prove to be compatible then they can later "confirm" their relationship in marriage (for the sake of the children) if they so choose. If they prove to be incompatible, then surely breaking up will be easier than if they were married, and can be done relatively quietly, whereas a marriage breakdown is far more visible and painful. And why should a piece of paper make any real difference?

The 'rightness' of cohabitation has, here in the Western world, become part of folklore, accepted by virtually all and questioned by few. It seems to be mainly the old-fashioned "fuddy duddies" of the church who are most exercised by sex outside marriage. Surely if people love each other then it is right that they should "make love".

And to do that in a stable relationship makes it even more appropriate to enter into that full relationship by living together. There is a sense in which society wants to consummate the marriage before it happens, and many people think that putting the proverbial "cart before the horse" does not matter so long as "love" is present. We will not waste too much time examining cohabitation. The fact of the matter is that the Maker's Instructions direct us to a one-flesh relationship with commitment being total and with no thought of dissolution in the event that circumstances change. The only word we have for such a *one flesh* relationship is *marriage* and that is the clear intention of God expressed throughout His Scriptures, both Old and New Testaments. The relationship is not a contract, it is a covenant in which God acts as witness, as we saw in Chapter 4. The Bible is silent on the ceremonial aspects of marriage. Surprising as it may seem, the Bible does not say we must marry in a church, nor that the woman shall wear white and the man a black top-hat. Nor does the Bible allude in any way to the duties of a Registrar or the issuance of a marriage licence. (These norms have developed over time in the Western World to place some certainty and legal rigour around the fact of marriage. We repeat, they are not scriptural ordinances).

Some will say that Christians are known to be against cohabitation, so that what they say can be discounted on that basis – as being a biased viewpoint. However there are compelling sociological studies that show the inherent weakness of cohabitation, both as a mechanism to create stable and long lasting relationships, and especially as a precursor to marriage. It seems once again that science (in this case social science) does seem to confirm the rightness of Scripture. If a reader wants to consult a non-Christian (and therefore supposedly independent) view on cohabitation then the best book is Patricia Morgan's *Marriage – Lite* published by The Institute for the Study of Civil Society (August 2000, ISBN 1-903386-0-4-7). In this study Professor Morgan shows that marriage and co-habitation are fundamentally different, and that one does not necessarily lead to the other. Cohabiting relationships are fragile and often short-lived, more likely to break up than marriages, regardless of age, income levels or social status. Surprisingly, cohabitations with children are more vulnerable than those without. Cohabitants are more likely to behave as single people than married people in terms of fidelity to partners, substance abuse and other health related behaviours. And the risk of violent and abusive behaviour is greater.

These are unwelcome conclusions, based on a vast array of sociological research from around the world. Needless to say *Marriage – Lite* was not a book that was favourably received by many sections of the UK media – in fact it seems they made a conscious effort to ignore it. Whilst a UK book, and with many of the statistics based on UK research, *Marriage – Lite* accesses sociological research globally and compares and contrasts data from most Western countries, finding common themes and common statistics emerging. Here are the key facts reported in the book:

- Cohabitations with children are more likely to fragment than those without.
- Couples who have children and then marry are more likely to divorce than couples who have children within marriage.
- The median duration of childless cohabitation is 19 months before it leads to birth, or marriage, or terminates.
- Half of female cohabitants under 60 live with their "partner" for less than two years, and only 16% for more than five years.
- Cohabitations described as 'stable unions' usually refer to ones that produce children – but fewer than one in ten women having their first child in cohabitation are still cohabiting ten years on – half will become lone parents.
- Poorer men tend not to marry. USA statistics show that wage rises tend to result in correlated marriage rises.
- Parents of cohabitees are less likely to transfer wealth to unmarried children.
- Means tested benefits may discourage marriage and encourage low-income people to keep unions "off the books" as these discriminate against married couples and make it financially worthwhile for people to operate as two singles, one with children.
- Women's ability to control pregnancy *may* have weakened men's feelings that they are morally obliged to marry their pregnant girlfriend.
- Men expect women to have uncommitted sex. If a

woman does not comply, both man and woman are aware he can go elsewhere – leaving women who expect marriage and children disadvantaged.

- A majority of children born to cohabitants are likely to spend time with a lone parent, as only 36% will live with both parents throughout childhood, compared to 70% of those born to married parents.
- As long term cohabitations are rare, and since cohabitations break up at a higher and faster rate than marriages, this leaves more people 'unpartnered'.
- Marriages preceded by cohabitation are less stable than those not preceded by cohabitation – even after marriage of 15 years, previously cohabiting couples appear to be 20% more likely to divorce after 15 years

We are all aware of the dangers of "lies, damned lies, and statistics" and the ease with which people with *an agenda* can select or manipulate data that supports their cause. It must be repeated that Professor Morgan's *Marriage – Lite* is based upon hundreds of national and international studies and full references for the statistics and context of statistics is provided in twenty-nine pages of references at the back of her book. The research results, however, seem quite intuitive and entirely consistent with the revelation of Scripture. Cohabitations do not help marriages, they hinder them, and the first five chapters of our book may well have suggested why this should be the case. That men value cohabitation even more lightly than women also seems intuitive. Perhaps the most poignant comment reported in *Marriage – Lite* in response to one of the studies cited by Professor Morgan was "Why buy a cow if you can get the milk for nothing?"

Cohabitation strikes against the Maker's Instructions that we reviewed in Chapter 1. Some might (weakly) argue that, in cohabiting, a man does indeed cleave to his 'wife', and possibly with the expectation of 'doing the decent thing by her' at a later stage, in marrying at some point. But how many people reading this book know personally people who have had one or more cohabitations and been seriously damaged by their break up? By mimicking the *one flesh* relationship, and by consummating in the flesh what has not been consummated in heaven (as it were), what permanent scars, what permanent fractures are left behind? We noted in Chapter 1 that the "fabric" of our lives is always impacted and scarred by the dislocation of a *one flesh* relationship.

As this book is not a social science book, and as most readers will not be interested in statistics, we will delve no further into Patricia Morgan's book. If readers are seriously challenged by what has been said, then the obvious next stopping point is to get a copy of her book (just £6 in August 2000). Another book in a similar vein is Rebecca O'Neill's *Does Marriage Matter?*, also written from a sociological viewpoint (published in the UK by *Civitas*, The Institute for the Study of Civil Society, ISBN 1-903 386-31 4 and just £2.50 when published in 2006). It draws similar conclusions within its fifty-one pages.

Violet Sammons, the mother of the author of this book, had a very homespun, simple and wise approach to cohabitation and sex outside marriage, the cool logic of which impressed me as a lad and has remained with me since. She used to say. "Peter, if you truly love a girl, then you'll wait for her. And if she truly loves you, then she will wait for you too." She also noted that if a couple truly loved each other then why on earth wouldn't they marry? And if they were unsure whether they truly loved each other, then they should not be living together or having sex with each other. Whilst the Bible nowhere says this in quite those terms, it seems to be a perfect summation of what the Lord has in mind in terms of a *one flesh* relationship. The commitment is once only and permanent. Should there be 'difficulties' later on, they are to be worked through first and foremost in a marriage context, where the preservation of the union is paramount. And my mother knew all about marriage difficulties, as I commented in the Introduction to this book!

Jesus on Cohabitation

Surprising as it may seem, the Lord Jesus said next to nothing on cohabitation. One reason for this is that the practice was much less prevalent in His society than it is today. It was not a big issue. But He did affirm what the Scriptures said about marriage and divorce, as we saw in chapter 1. Then, as now, adultery was considered as worse than fornication, and the sanctity of marriage was uppermost in the minds of all. There is, however, one account that is found only in the Gospel of John (the Gospels being the four biographies of Jesus found in the New Testament, namely: Matthew, Mark, Luke and John). This is the account of His conversation with the Samaritan woman at the well at the town of Sychar. (See John 4: 1–41 for the whole story.)

That Jesus should have had a conversation at all with an unaccompanied woman was remarkable in the social context of the day. That it should have been with one of the Samaritans (whom most Jews detested) was even more remarkable. And that the woman herself was most likely a social outcast (forced to draw water at midday when there were no other women around) made it more remarkable still. Normally a woman would be ignored, and a social outcast would be shunned at all costs, but Jesus was different. His agenda was healing – healing of bodies, minds, relationships, and above all, healing of the fractured relationship between men (and women) and God.

There are a range of truths and lessons in His conversation with the woman, and that is why readers may want to follow the entire account, to get a clearer picture of what was afoot in their discussion together. Jesus was introducing the reality that what He offers to the world is a cleansing stream of "living water" that cannot be exhausted – that water of *forgiveness* of past sins and of *new life* lived in Him; a "water" that will be, for the person who "drinks" of it, eternal life itself. Here is a fully satisfying "water" that will well-up from inside, not from outside. It is notable that this account of the unlikely and unprecedented conversation with an outcast woman from an outcast ethnic group, in John chapter 4, should follow on directly from chapter 3 where Jesus has stated that no one can "see" the kingdom of God unless he (or she!) is born again. "**Do not be surprised**" said Jesus "**because I tell you that you must all be born again**" (John 3: 7). We pick up the thread for our purposes at 4: 15.

John 4: 15–19
"Sir," the woman said, "give me that water! Then I will never be thirsty again, nor will I have to come here to draw water."

"Go and call your husband," Jesus told her, "and come back."

"I don't have a husband," she answered.

Jesus replied, "You are right when you say you don't have a husband. You have been married to five men, and the man you live with now is not really your husband. You have told me the truth."

"I see you are a prophet, sir," the woman said.

The woman takes Jesus' comment about water welling up from inside in a literal sense, although whether in fact she was being a little sarcastic or disbelieving we cannot say from the evidence we have. But the Lord's instruction cuts right to the quick – go and call your husband. This lady was a serial cohabiter, on her sixth "husband" as far as we can make out. Her reputation as a lady of easy virtue was probably the reason why she was an outcast – other women probably ignored her, and going to draw water when other women were around was just too painful. Of course Jesus could have avoided her pain altogether and just said something like, "God will forgive you if you trust in Him and live in accordance with his laws". But Jesus knows her needs are deeper than that and so He confronts the key dislocation of her life. She has been "one flesh" at least six times with different "partners" (to use the modern term) and this has left deep scars. She is "lost" in this particular lifestyle and can see no way out. Her way of dealing with the pain is to lead a reclusive life as far as she possibly can. It is tragic. She will be like this, leading a twilight life, for the rest of her years. But Jesus is the great healer of tragedies and He is not prepared to leave her in this state. "Go and call your husband" is a challenge. Jesus knows the root of the problem.

In verse 20 the woman immediately changes the subject and seeks to enter into a religious discourse on some minor religious controversy. How often we hide behind "religion" to avoid the direct questions of Jesus. Jesus duly allows her to change the subject, His point having already been made. The real lesson He wants her to take away is in verses 23-4: **"The time is coming – and is already here – when by the power of God's Spirit people will worship the Father *as he really is*, offering him the true worship that he wants. God is Spirit, and only by the power of his Spirit can people worship him *as he really is*."** This woman needs God's power to live aright – and so do we all. What was true for the Samaritan woman, this outcast, two thousand years ago, is true for us today. All we who are outcasts and have not asked Jesus for His living water to clean up our lives and empower us to live for Him, desperately need His "water", just as does a parched throat that needs to drink much water in the noonday sun. Her need was desperate. Our need is desperate.

John chapter 4 is Jesus' only reference to cohabitation and what is sometimes today called 'serial monogamy'. Jesus knew it was injurious. Whatever "love" the woman had found with husband number one was insufficient. As it was to be insufficient with the next five "husbands". She had been one flesh in a physical sense six times and still she knew no peace, rather the reverse. This lady had ignored the Maker's Instructions and led life as she saw fit. That life carried significant consequences and real emotional pain. But the outcome, now that Jesus was on the scene, was to be a joyous one! It seems that the woman took on board what Jesus had said and believed (verses 39–42). Not only did she believe, she influenced others to believe too. It may well be that from being an outcast she became a celebrated friend and spiritual mother figure within her community. And no doubt like others to whom Jesus ministered, with God's strength she was able to put right the things in her life that she knew were wrong. We wonder whether, like the woman caught in adultery (John 8: 1–11), Jesus' loving instruction to the woman of Sychar was, quietly, "go and sin no more".

We can only observe, then, that the *one flesh* ordinance from God is undermined by cohabitation, and indeed any such false "consummation" damages our ability to enter into that wonderful relationship for us that God has planned. How do we then deal with a situation where we have "consummated" a marriage before being married, possibly including open cohabitation, and subsequently come to the conclusion that it was a "mistake" (to put it very politely)? In the light of what Jesus taught, and of what the Bible clearly teaches about two becoming *one flesh*, how can we deal with the situation of having "given away" the gift that was meant for our life partner? Forgiveness lies at the heart of biblical Christianity and at the heart of Jesus' mission. There is no sin that is beyond forgiveness (except one, and sexual impurity is not that one). God has acted with *agape* love singularly in the New Testament in giving His Son Jesus for all people who will repent of their sins (stop doing them, and turn away from them) and believe in Jesus. They can have a living relationship with Him. His arms are opened wide to embrace them, just as Jesus' arms were opened wide on the cross of execution. It is a shame, literally and metaphorically, to have given away the gift of becoming "one" when that gift is given to one who is not our life's intended – in some way it dishonours our future wife or husband – a person we may not yet even have met. Can a successful relationship be entered into when we carry this particular burden of guilt and sadness?

The answer is yes. The indelible stain can be eradicated and we can be prepared once again for a true *one flesh* relationship. But the matter must be dealt with. The sin must be recognised as such and then confessed as such. Confession is between the penitent sinner and God through Jesus, not through any "intermediary" such as a priest. The nub of the matter is confession, so we read: **If we confess our sins, he is faithful and just**

and will forgive us our sins and purify us from all unrighteousness. If we claim we have not sinned, we make him out to be a liar and his word has no place in our lives (1 John 1: 9–10 NIV). Some disclosure to our future spouse may also be necessary. In this, utmost wisdom is required but the good news is that a seeker after truth is not alone. The Holy Spirit will give you wisdom in this *if you ask Him*. So forgiveness is possible and essential if the sin is not to carry through into, and spoil, any future relationship. This is not to say that the former sin carries no consequence: sadly not all consequences can be eliminated. Where they endure, some allowance for that endurance must be made. One key element of this that is often forgotten is that, once we have been forgiven by God, we need to learn to *accept and really believe that we have been forgiven*. (Some writers call this "forgiving ourselves" but that usage tends to suggest, wrongly, that we don't need to repent *toward God* for having offended against *Him*.) As time goes by, pain inevitably lessens and a true seeker after God will have other compensating blessings poured into his or her life. So we do need to learn to let go of our past and keep our eyes fixed upon Jesus (Hebrews 12: 2).

Jesus' final words to us as He releases us with His penetrating, loving gaze, is always summed up by the words "go and sin no more". There are two parts to Jesus' statement in John chapter 8 which we need to bear in mind; "neither do I condemn you" and "go and sin no more". The historical church has often been guilty of emphasising the latter and ignoring the former! But parts of the modern church are inclined to reverse the fault – to emphasise forgiveness and to tell us there is no need to change our behaviour – indeed in parts of the "liberal church" things that were once understood as sins are now celebrated as virtues. But Jesus' gentle command was and is "go and sin no more" (John 8: 11). He is interested in our future being better than our past!

Jesus on Divorce

We have already seen in Chapter 1 that the Lord's attitude to divorce was uncompromising. Rather than expend further pages of text on adultery, divorce and marriage, readers are encouraged to undertake their own private Bible study on those questions if they think that more emphasis is needed. The key texts on adultery, divorce, and marriage in terms of the afterlife are these:

Adultery
Matthew 5: 27–30

Adultery/Fornication
1 Corinthians 6: 18–20; 1 Corinthians 7: 1–5.

Divorce
Matthew 5: 31 – 32 [See also Matthew 19: 1–12; Mark 10: 11–12; Luke 16: 18]

Marriage
Matthew 22: 23–33 [See also Mark 12: 18–27; Luke 20: 27–40]

These texts are pretty self-explanatory, especially in terms of what we have discovered in the first 5 chapters of this book. I will just comment however, on Jesus' statement in Matthew 5: 28, where he declares that looking at a woman lustfully (or as the Good News Translation has it – anyone who looks at a woman and *wants to possess her*) is the same as committing adultery. This is perhaps for many men one of the most alarming declarations that Jesus made on any subject. Plainly it is possible to sin in the mind as much as in the flesh – which is one reason why pornography is so destructive. What Jesus said about men applies as much to women, although they seem rather less prone to this particular sin – women are quite right in saying that there is an equality issue at play here! However, Jesus addresses the statement to men, and in this we might be seeing the fact that as God's appointed head of the household (no matter what failings he may have), it is the man that will be judged first on these and other issues.

So are we guilty if we just "fancy" someone in the street – perhaps an unguarded and fleeting appreciation of female beauty that went a little bit too far? John White in his best selling *Eros Defiled* (ISBN 0-85110-407-X, sub-titled "The Problem of Sexual Guilt", pub. 1985) thought the answer was no. It all depends on what Jesus meant by "lustful" or wanting to "possess" the woman. What Jesus probably meant was that that the man's decision to hold the woman in his mind and think of her inappropriately is what is equivalent to adultery. A fleeting fancy, even if quite coarse in nature, is surely not what He meant. But a decision to think about someone, especially a neighbour, a work colleague, someone at school or otherwise known to us socially and personally, in a positively lustful way has transgressed the *one flesh* ordinance. Our bodies may have been faithful, but our minds have not. Or, as the fictional character Rhett Butler said of Ashley Wilkes in the film *Gone with the Wind*, "Poor Mr Wilkes. He cannot be physically unfaithful to his wife, but he cannot be mentally faithful to her either". And just for the record, as someone once asked the author directly about it, Jesus does not literally mean us to pluck out an eye if we transgress in this area! Otherwise we would have a virtually blind male population in a few weeks! Clearly Jesus means that this deadly sin of the mind has to be dealt with most radically (in the heart – in our mind, where that sin originates) otherwise the sin will ultimately destroy us. It is truly that serious, or the Lord Jesus would not have said it.

Where is the Old Liar in this?

That marriage has enemies scarcely needs to be said. But we have to reflect that it is Satan who has the biggest stake in undermining marriage. Since the sexual urge is universal, so the misuse of the sexual urge is a universally useful weapon against mankind. The devil wants to prosecute his war against God, albeit he knows his time is rapidly running out. As God loves His people, to seek to injure God the devil injures people. And one of his tactics is to pervert the natural desire into an unnatural one – the good and wholesome desire for relationship in all its dimensions, including the one flesh dimension, is just too great an opportunity for Satan to miss. What God saw as good in Genesis chapters 1 and 2, the devil spoils. Can *we* resist the devil's wiles in this area? The answer is certainly yes, but not in our own strength. We must ask for God's help, and in particular for the infilling of His Holy Spirit, Who both cleanses and empowers us to live for God the Father.

It is always, always, always marriage that is first in line for attack. This is because it reflects the relationship that Jesus has with his church, and that is a relationship of which the devil is extremely jealous. The devil wants us to worship him, whether knowingly or unknowingly, and he hates the devotion of the Bridegroom (Christ) for his Bride (the church). It might be added that the devil hates happy and stable families and wants to injure them. It is injured people in injured relationships that he is best able to control, and control is the name of his game. But we always remind ourselves as Christians that *He who is in us is greater than he who is in the world*. (1 John 4: 4)

On this matter of attacks upon marriage, it is noteworthy that everywhere marriage is under attack. Historically, two attacks on the institution of marriage that took on an absolutely industrial scale were those launched by the French and Russian Revolutions. A quick Google search will reveal most of what interested readers may want to know, but for interest let us see what each revolution had in store for the institution of marriage and how each Revolution eventually had to be curtailed in this area:

The French Revolution and Marriage

Many voices had arisen before 1789 ("the Great French Revolution") to claim freedom to divorce. The French church had a lock on divorce law, and divorce was virtually impossible to obtain. During the years 1789–1790, at least twenty books and pamphlets were published in France on the question of divorce. The text of the new constitution, adopted in August 1791, recognised marriage as a non-religious contract, whilst remaining silent on divorce. Irrespective of this silence many individuals took the new constitution as the green light to divorce before a notary and to remarry before their municipality. It is interesting how attempts to redefine marriage so often open the floodgate to all sorts of changes purportedly "not foreseen" by the legislators.

In 1792 the revolution entered a far more radical phase. Immediately divorce became lawful and universal male suffrage was brought in. Love of "freedom" was noted in the preamble to the divorce law of 1792: "The National Assembly considering how important it is to give the French access to divorce, which being a right contingent on individual freedom would be frustrated by an indissoluble bond...." The preamble went on to state that the right to divorce rested on two basic principles: whoever wishes to divorce must be able to do so, and the municipalities should not have to consider the legitimacy of the reasons which caused the desire for rupture. In other words divorce on demand, no questions asked. The legal requirements were to be least restricted where there was clear mutual consent. In these situations the couple were to call a family meeting of at least three friends or relatives chosen by each partner, who were to try to encourage the couple to stay together. If this failed then the couple, after one month cooling-off, were to present themselves to the municipality for the divorce to be progressed without investigation of its causes.

The formalities required to obtain divorce pronounced against one partner were not very complicated either. There were a number of officially recognised reasons for divorce – insanity, crimes or maltreatment by one against the other, a custodial sentence, known immoral behaviour, abandonment for more than two years, the absence of one without news for more than five years. Politicians were very pleased with these new arrangements. Chaumette in October 1792 said, "Divorce is the father of mutual regard, of kindness, of caring, permanent nutrients of true passion ..... the spirit guide of nuptial bond, since it permits enjoyment of indestructible peace and uninterrupted happiness". In August 1793 Citizen Noah wrote in the *Convention* that "marriage and divorce are constraints; indeed can't we create excellent citizens, without the law interfering in their sexual relationships? Should Man, to whom the author of things gave the pleasures of love to charm heavy cares, be less privileged than the other animals which freely follow their natural instincts?"

The French church complained that the new laws

opened up the way to polygamy. They were right. Citizen Fleurant addressed a petition to the *Convention* in 1793. He argued "The Rights of Man permit any act which does not harm others .... but is this really so? How does slavery and the barbaric practice of ancient despotism requiring that a man marry only one woman continue to exist?" Citizen Dhenin protested before the same *Convention* that he had earned a six-year prison sentence for bigamy: "A marriage is without rights if one spouse may dissolve it by a simple act of will." Why then, he asked, was he to be sent to prison simply because he had neglected to divorce? He was condemned, he said "for a mere formality". It is sadly ironic how "modern" and "contemporary" some of these French revolutionary ideas sound today!

Due to the obvious dangers of divorce-on-demand, with the ready abandonment of women and children and the inevitable casting of these victims onto some form of public aid for the destitute, it was not long before the legislators began to roll back the "advances" of the Revolution. We should perhaps not be too surprised at the extremities of the anti marriage party – all this occurred during what has been termed in France *The Terror*, where Madame Guillotine held sway and people were killed in their multiple thousands. In 1816 divorce was abolished with the restoration of the monarchy.

The Russian Revolution and Marriage

When the Bolsheviks came to power in 1917 they regarded the family, like every other "bourgeois" institution, with fierce hatred, and set out to destroy it. One of the first decrees of the Soviet government was to abolish the term "illegitimate" child. This was achieved simply by equalising the legal status of all children, whether born in or out of wedlock. The Soviets were able to boast that Russia was the only country with no illegitimate children. At the same time a law was passed that enabled divorce in a few minutes, at the request of either party. On 20th December 1917 the first decree on marriage was issued, by which from then on the republic recognised *only* civil marriages – thus removing the church from involvement. As with the French Revolution some 124 years earlier, laws were passed that enabled dissolution of marriage by mutual consent of the parties or at the request of one of them. Abortion on demand was also facilitated.

The result was chaos. Men took to changing their wives with the changing seasons. Some were reported to have harems of twenty or more wives – with the inevitable offspring often thrown out onto the streets. Needless to say these children became brutalised and criminalised. Young peasant men at the age of twenty might have four wives. Young women of the same age might by then have experienced four abortions. In 1926 a new Code of Marriage Laws was enacted which "liberalised" matters still more. There was now no necessity of obligatory registration. Unregistered cohabitations created the same legal consequences as a marriage. Registration was still considered to be in the interests of the State and of the parties by providing evidence of married status, but was not a condition of marriage. To divorce, even the formal hearing of a divorce was no longer necessary – only registration with the Department of Civil Status. The minimum age for marriage, however, was raised to eighteen for both parties. Pre-nuptial property remained separate and protected, but post-marriage property was shared equally.

The Soviet State, in anticipation of the coming war with Germany, and after massive butchery of the Russian population as a consequence of the onward march of the Revolution in the 1920s and 1930s, in the very early 1940s became more interested in protecting the institution of marriage with a view to increasing the population. In April 1944 couples were officially encouraged to register unregistered cohabitations so as to acquire marriage rights and crucially the State declared that "only registered marriage creates the rights and duties of spouses". The unregistered cohabitations of 1926 were finally done away with. By 1946 it was officially confirmed that the Soviet State was striving to reinforce family ties. Sadly, it was the exigencies of war that led to the reinvigoration of marriage in Russia, not the recognition of the moral implications of the feral, cohabiting society that had been created by the Revolution. By the decree of 8 July, 1944 there was increased help for expectant mothers, increased protection of mothers and children, and the creation of orders of 'Heroine Mother' and of 'Motherhood Glory' complete with *Medals of Motherhood* to be given to mothers of large families. In addition there was an imposition of taxes on bachelors, childless couples and those couples with only a few children. Children were effectively seen as the property of the State, something that can only be achieved in totalitarian societies, with the child-bearing population as a giant baby factory.

So where was the Old Liar in all this? We can speculate that Satan was intimately involved in the evils of both the French and Russian Revolutions. One can only wonder at the hundreds of thousands, if not millions, of unhappy lives that were created by these two crazy experiments with the status of marriage, and the fact that in both cases the children of so many unhappy unions became the cannon fodder for the State's "defence" of its political interest, as in the Napoleonic wars and in the so-called Great Patriotic War between Nazism and Communism. It can only be repeated once again, the devil hates marriage because it is a God-ordinance, and a foundational ordinance in Genesis, meant for the good of mankind and leading to the taming of the world in accordance with God's good plan. Was it altogether a coincidence that the so-called swinging sixties were also known as the Sexual Revolution? Marriage will always be under attack.

*"Happy are those who have been invited
to the wedding feast"*

7

GENIUS

Is God a "spoilsport"?

**There are three things that are too amazing for me,
four that I do not understand:
the way of an eagle in the sky,
the way of a snake on a rock,
the way of a ship on high seas,
and the way of a man with a maiden**

This is from the book of Proverbs in the Old Testament, that collection of moral and religious teachings in the form of sayings or 'proverbs' (see Proverbs 30: 18–19). Much of the book has to do with practical, everyday concerns. It begins with a reminder of the value of wisdom and tells us that to have knowledge (in the sense of wisdom) one must have reverence for the Lord. In the previous six chapters of *One Flesh* we have sought to understand the mind of the Lord for men and women in relation to each other. This surely is a very sensible thing to do as the vast majority of us expect to form relationships as we go through life, and especially where these relationships are between a man and a woman, we want them to be happy and mutually beneficial. As we said in the Introduction to this book, no one enters a relationship for it to go wrong; no one gets married in order to live miserably. And yet very often we do seem to go about this whole matter of "relationship forming" in a way that seems perversely guaranteed to weaken the relationship even before it has got started! The passage from Proverbs quoted above, using its inimitable dry wit, really rams home this point as between men and women! There are indeed four things that are both amazing and difficult to understand. An eagle flying in the sky: we cannot tell its mind, nor where it will fly to next. A snake slithering across a hot rock: we do not know where it has come from nor where it is going. A ship tossed around by winds and currents: we cannot tell the precise course that it will take. And finally – a man with a maiden.... How often we see young men (and sometimes older men) making a spectacle of themselves trying to impress women! If a man makes a fool of himself in the pursuit of a "maiden", we just don't know precisely how things will end – except that they will end, in all probability, with the trashing of the man's reputation. Where relationship-forming is our objective, we too often let go of common sense! And yet the Designer of men and women really does want us to live happily ever after – and happily with each other! That is His good design. That is His good purpose. The Maker's Instructions give us plenty of good guidance as to how we should behave as we contemplate a one-flesh relationship.

Where Jesus speaks about male and female relationships, His teaching is, without exception, consistent with the Scriptures of His day (what we call the Old Testament). But Jesus' teaching is always highly practical in its implications, which can make it uncomfortable reading! So, for example, the Proverbs speak about adultery, about its true cost and the wisdom of resisting its temptations. Rather than cover more pages here with extracts from the Bible, I encourage readers to check out Proverbs 6: 20–35 and Proverbs 7: 1–27. You may want to pause and do that now.

What did Jesus *add* to this teaching? He affirmed it and brought to it a shocking practicality as we saw in our previous chapter – that a man who so much as looks at a woman lustfully is guilty of sin in his heart (see Matthew 5: 27–32). So much of Jesus' practical teaching was contained in what we call the "Sermon on the Mount", which is actually Matthew chapters 5, 6 and 7 inclusive. If readers want to get a real sense of Jesus' teaching across the full spectrum of subjects – what some have called Jesus' manifesto – then again you may want to pause, sit down with a Bible and read through those three chapters for yourself. There are no words that I can add that bring this any more alive – it is best to read it direct.

Why are the teachings of the Bible so often directed towards men? Are women "let off the hook" as regards sexual temptation? As suggested in chapter 4 there is an order of priority in which God will be seeking answers for the conduct of a marriage. The man will answer first (and foremost) and the wife only secondly, but that does not mean she has a lesser responsibility for her conduct. But let's face it, all too often it is the man that goes astray, and woe betide him if he has not got a good answer when God demands an explanation – as He assuredly will. The Bible's attitude to women reveals a positive and a high expectation: Proverbs 14: 1 – **Homes are made by the wisdom of women, but are destroyed by foolishness**. The wisdom of the woman is seen as a godly gift, but again this does not excuse a man for being unwise in the conduct of his household or family affairs. A man should seek a good wife and seek to encourage her and build her up. Apart from affirming the *one flesh* nature of God's plan for men and women, Jesus' teaching was clearly opposed to the ease with which a man might "get rid of" his wife through divorce. In addition He affirmed that marriage does not survive into the hereafter – in other words we do not stay married when we go to heaven (see Matthew 22: 23–33 and Romans 7: 1–3 for a comment by the Apostle Paul on the same subject). We turn shortly to the teaching of the apostles in the letters of Paul to obtain further practical guidance.

In the light of all that we have explored in this book, some readers may still perversely (in the light of the noble intentions of God as regards *one flesh*) have the impression that God is a killjoy in this area of sex and relationships. After all, He created us and presumably placed within us the powerful sex instinct. Is it not "unreasonable" of Him to expect us to refrain from sexual encounters until we are ready for a marriage (one flesh) relationship? Such a question probably betrays an untrusting attitude to God, which is probably not the attitude to adopt in trying to find an answer! But let us consider this for just a moment. If God had not placed within us a very powerful urge first to form relationships and second to consummate them physically, then would we have fulfilled God's prime directive to mankind: **have many children, so that your descendants will live all over the earth and bring it under their control** (Genesis 1: 28)? The prime directive could not have been fulfilled except by men and women working together, impelled by the wholesome appetite that God had placed in them. If these appetites were not powerful, then mankind would have failed. But the strong instincts were placed in us with a view to them being explored within a relationship as set out by the Maker.

Why then does God take such an apparently hard line on how we behave? Is it perhaps because of the possibility for the spread of STDs (sexually transmitted diseases)? This may have something to do with it but is not the primary reason. Is it because of the strong possibility for the breakdown of those relationships that are so dear to God's heart? This also may have something to do with it but is not the primary reason. Is it because people get hurt (sometimes terribly hurt) when relationships break down? This may once again have something to do with it but is not the primary reason. Is it because of unwanted pregnancies with all that these imply? Once again we have to say that may have something to do with it but is not the primary reason. The primary reason why God has commanded a *one flesh* relationship and sexual abstinence outside of that relationship is that *this is the sort of relationship that can best nurture children*.

Any child born into this world will have a soul – which, through whatever circumstances life may bring, will ultimately make a choice, either for relationship with the Saviour, or a choice against the Saviour.

We recognize that many single parent families do their utmost for the children, teaching them about Jesus, and that is wonderful to see. Like all parents they need love and encouragement from other believers.

There is surely no greater tragedy than that any child should be born to parents unwilling or simply unable to bring it up to know its Lord. We have been given the gift of physical relationships for expression within a *one flesh* context. No greater tragedy? To engage in physical relationships in any other context is ultimately selfish. To risk a new soul being created that may well find itself un-nurtured, and so not taught about its Lord and its Saviour and its need of a saving relationship, but possibly instead being a child neglected and possibly even to know that it was unwanted – these are true tragedies.

Some might then say that it matters less if they "take precautions", and that if a child unexpectedly results, they would nurture their offspring, perhaps even trying to give him or her a "religious understanding". That is to miss entirely the point about the sanctity of marriage and the need for leaving and cleaving. Some might try to argue that unmarried sexual relations matter less if the partners are too old to bear children, but in the same way that is also to miss the point. Far from being a spoilsport, God is a the Heavenly Father who wants the absolute best for the individuals that make up His creation. He knows what is best for us and has spelled it out for us in the Maker's Instructions. Is sexual sin the worst sort of sin? Many Christian commentators have argued the answer is "no". But all sin has consequences, and the consequences of sexual sin seem more far-reaching than many sins that we might name. God puts in place restrictions not because He is a killjoy but because His will is the best. He knows what is best for His people. And we have seen how much He loved us because He sent His Son Jesus to die in our place and rise again so that we may live in Him.

"But surely we are just animals...?"

If readers have been paying attention so far in this book, it hopefully will not have escaped their notice that in God's eyes we are not "just" anything. We are His special creation, meant for relationship with Himself – and with each other. That human male and female were designed *for* each other is a fact that scarcely needs to be laboured. Men and women are the same, yet different. Their physiques are complementary – we think of the angularity of the male physique and the curves of the female. The physical adjacency of the procreative organs between male and female suggests they were meant for each other. The point is sometimes made that the animals mate, but humans, in the right context, "make love". It was pop star Tina Turner whose 1980s song carried the refrain "What's love got to do with it?" The answer is: absolutely everything! Adam was bowled over by Eve, and we see the joy of his realisation as she is brought to him by God (Genesis 2: 23). That is the joyful relationship that God desires for all of us, or at least those who are not definitely called to the joys of singleness. But we repeat, humans "make love" face to face. The idea of tenderness, of love, of joy, are to be known to humans in the right context. Animals almost universally mate front to back. Relationship is not "special" to them in the same way as to humans – they are not created in the likeness of God. (Some people point out that certain species of whale and one species of monkey mate front to front, but these would seem to be the exceptions that prove the rule. We cannot imagine whales gazing lovingly into each other's eyes!)

Yes, animals in their lives will have potentially numerous mates; relatively few tend to be monogamous. God's plan for humans is monogamy. Where there are instructions given for the treatment of second wives in the Bible these are provided because God recognises the sinfulness of mankind (of men!). Throughout the Bible the joys of monogamy are promoted and we scarcely need to repeat that Jesus affirmed the rightness of this approach. The world tries to tell us that polygamy in one form or another is "good", whether in legally recognised forms or in the common Western sense of serial "shacking up". Some of the world's non Judeo-Christian faiths teach the same – we think for example of temporary marriage, or *mutah* marriage, as practised in Islam. We have noted previously that science sometimes inadvertently confirms the rightness of God's instructions. As regards the practice of polygamy, it is the science of economics that seems to confirm God's plans. The UK *Financial Times* (1st February, 2005) carried an interesting report ***Economic Theories Reveal the Pitfalls of Polygamy***. A study published by the Centre for Economic Policy Research argued that mass polygamy can make it hard for economies "to break out of the poverty trap". The practice, it said, allowed rich men to spend their wealth on wife "quantity" rather than investing in child quality. The study quoted in the Financial Times was based on detailed research on the Ivory Coast of Africa. There, four in ten women of child bearing age shared husbands.

Richer men tended to have more wives, but richer men who were well educated or earned their income from wages tended to have fewer wives. Rich men who earned their income from other sources – land or corruption – tended to have more wives. The study showed that educated men have an interest in finding "quality" wives of good education because they have more chance of producing a skilled and well-educated child with high earning potential. Quality wives, like any other commodity, come at a higher price and so a man will be able to afford fewer of them. But rich men whose success is not rooted in education have less chance of producing a well-educated child – the best way of maximising income is to produce many children and this requires multiple wives. The trouble with this approach is that it creates a large, poorly educated and so less productive population that must be fed. That in turn leads to increased individual poverty and acts as a drag on whole societies. The authors of the report recommended that governments in poorer countries should subsidise education more heavily. By creating a link between the division of a country's wealth and human capital, this would encourage men to find a single well-educated woman rather than a large number of wives. Whilst the primary purpose of God's *one flesh* ordinance is the blessing of individual men and women, and their offspring, we have to conclude that He also foresees the tragic "costs" of polygamy, whether they be economic or emotional.

The New Testament does not speak a great deal about polygamy. Where it does, it is only in a negative sense as these extracts show:

1 Timothy 3: 2

A church leader must be without fault; he must have only one wife, be sober, self-controlled, and orderly; he must welcome strangers in his home; he must be able to teach....

1 Timothy 3: 12

A church helper must have only one wife, and be able to manage his children and family well.

Titus 1: 6

An elder must be without fault; he must have only one wife, and his children must be believers and not have the reputation of being wild or disobedient.

It was recognised in the early church that where a convert to Christianity had come from a pagan background and had been engaged in polygamy, the husband should provide for his other wives but be *one flesh* with just one. There was no need to labour the point, precisely because monogamy was the Jewish style, ordained by God and inherited by the church. For those people, especially church people, who believe that all religions are essentially one and that God ordained them all, there is an interesting problem for them to explain away: why does their "god" allow some religions to practise polygamy and legislates in others against polygamy? A problem indeed!

Paul and the *one flesh* ordinance

Whilst Jesus taught relatively little about God's *one flesh* ordinance, besides affirming it, He elsewhere taught much about life in the Kingdom of God and of what God requires of those who seek to follow Him. The principles set out elsewhere in Scripture are consistent with what Jesus taught – gainsayers would need to "prove" from the Bible that Jesus taught something else! Jesus left the development of the church in the hands of the apostles (an *apostle* being from the New Testament Greek *apostolos* – one sent, or an emissary) who are today recognised almost universally as God's chosen leaders for the worldwide church that was initiated following the resurrection and ascension of Jesus. Of all the apostles it is Paul to whom we owe the greatest debt in setting down kingdom principles. It is rightly said that his letters to the various new churches and individuals taken together constitute the most thorough and deliberate theological formulations in the New Testament. So what did Paul teach about one flesh, relationships and sex outside of marriage?

Paul confirmed what the Lord Jesus had already taught regarding marriage in the hereafter – it does not exist:

Romans 7: 1–3

The law rules over people only as long as they live. A married woman, for example, is bound by the law to her husband as long as he lives; but if he dies, then she is free from the law that bound her to him. So then, if she lives with another man while her husband is alive, she will be called an adulteress; but if her husband dies, she is legally a free woman and does not commit adultery if she marries another man.

Regarding questions that had arisen within the Corinthian church about marriage, readers should check out 1 Corinthians chapter 7 in its entirety. In this chapter Paul speaks of the benefits of remaining single, but recommends that those who struggle with sexual temptation will be wise to marry. There is so much in this key chapter, we will leave readers to make their own private study and possibly, if they are so minded, to seek out other commentaries on 1 Corinthians 7, as there is just so much that needs to be considered and prayerfully worked-through. We have already seen that Paul affirmed monogamy (1 Timothy 3: 2; 1 Timothy 3: 12; Titus 1: 6).

In his letter to the Ephesians Paul states that among Christians there should not even be a hint of sexual immorality. Plainly then, Paul sees such immorality as injurious to individuals and to the body of Christ (the church). Instead we should try to imitate the Lord Jesus. Ephesians 5: 1–21 stands as a helpful guideline and warning to believers living in a sexually hostile environment (such as the Western world in this twenty-first century):

Since you are God's dear children, you must try to be like him. Your life must be controlled by love, just as Christ loved us and gave his life for us as a sweet-smelling offering and sacrifice that pleases God. Since you are God's people, it is not right that any matters of sexual immorality or indecency or greed should even be mentioned among you. Nor is it fitting for you to use language which is obscene, profane, or vulgar. Rather you should give thanks to God. You may be sure that no one who is immoral, indecent, or greedy (for greed is a form of idolatry) will ever receive a share in the Kingdom of Christ and of God. Do not let anyone deceive you with foolish words; it is because of these very things that God's anger will come upon those who do not obey him. So have nothing at all to do with such people. You yourselves used to be in the darkness, but since you have become the Lord's people, you are in the light. So you must live like people who belong to the light, for it is the light that brings a rich harvest of every kind of goodness, righteousness, and truth. Try to learn what pleases the Lord. Have nothing to do with the worthless things that people do, things that belong to the darkness. Instead, bring them out to the light. (It is really too shameful even to talk about the things they do in secret.) And when all things are brought out to the light, then their true nature is clearly revealed; for anything that is clearly

revealed becomes light. That is why it is said, "Wake up, sleeper, and rise from death, and Christ will shine on you." So be careful how you live. Don't live like ignorant people, but like wise people. Make good use of every opportunity you have, because these are evil days. Don't be fools, then, but try to find out what the Lord wants you to do. Do not get drunk with wine, which will only ruin you; instead, be filled with the Spirit. Speak to one another with the words of psalms, hymns, and sacred songs; sing hymns and psalms to the Lord with praise in your hearts. In the name of our Lord Jesus Christ, always give thanks for everything to God the Father. Submit yourselves to one another because of your reverence for Christ.

We will conclude this brief excursion into the writings of the Apostle Paul with his key teaching in 1 Corinthians chapter 6. His letter to the Corinthian church deals with problems of life and faith encountered by these believers in a city that had become a byword for moral corruption and sexual licence. Corinth was a great cosmopolitan Greek city, capital of the Roman province of Achaia. It was noted for its variety of religions, its culture, appalling immorality and heady commercial power – a city, perhaps, much like modern London!

1 Corinthians 6: 12–20
Someone will say, "I am allowed to do anything." Yes; but not everything is good for you. I could say that I am allowed to do anything, but I am not going to let anything make me its slave. Someone else will

say, "Food is for the stomach, and the stomach is for food." Yes; but God will put an end to both. The body is not to be used for sexual immorality, but to serve the Lord; and the Lord provides for the body. God raised the Lord from death, and he will also raise us by his power. You know that your bodies are parts of the body of Christ. Shall I take a part of Christ's body and make it part of the body of a prostitute? Impossible! Or perhaps you don't know that the man who joins his body to a prostitute becomes physically one with her? The scripture says quite plainly, "The two will become one body." But he who joins himself to the Lord becomes spiritually one with him. Avoid immorality. Any other sin a man commits does not affect his body; but the man who is guilty of sexual immorality sins against his own body. Don't you know that your body is the temple of the Holy Spirit, who lives in you and who was given to you by God? You do not belong to yourselves but to God; he bought you for a price. So use your bodies for God's glory.

We can see, then, that the temptation to sexual licence had become a problem in the early Corinthian church. What does Paul say, and how is it relevant today? Following Paul's ideas in sequence; it appears that some were saying that the organs of their bodies that were meant for sex should be used in that way – "food is for the stomach", they said. Paul agrees with them but his agreement is double-edged. He points out straight away that God will sooner or later "put an end" to both food and stomach. In the same way He will put an end, sooner or later, to our own bodies, complete with their sexual organs. But it is possible that Paul was also affirming that indeed sexual organs are to be used in a proper way for "food is for the stomach and the stomach for food". The unspoken truth being that the sexual organs are designed for the *one flesh* relationship between man and woman, and not to be used for other, perverted purposes. Our physical bodies, at least if we are believers, are *in Christ*, so should not be abused. Sexual immorality affects our own bodies, so we need to be aware of the consequence of choosing to abuse our bodies – there are physical consequences and there are spiritual consequences. To have sex with a "prostitute" involves the two becoming *one*, in a perverted mimicry of the *one flesh* ordinance. When two people mate who are out of wedlock, something happens at the profound spiritual level that makes them, albeit temporarily *one*, but without the necessary leaving and cleaving that is the only bedrock upon which love can truly be built. For non-Christians this sin is bad enough and carries inevitable consequences, but for Christians it is fatal, in the sense that it destroys our ability to live and to witness for Jesus. It can even destroy our salvation.

The Genius of Marriage

Whilst the world at large teaches sexual freedom and tells us that we are missing out if we are not sexually active, Jesus affirmed the truly revolutionary idea that man and woman are designed for a *one flesh* relationship. This book is not a "how to" manual, nor is its writer an "agony uncle", capable of providing specific advice to singles or couples. There are others who are better placed to provide guidance in these areas. One relatively recent book that readers may want to get hold of is (Australian) Dr Martin Panter's *Deluded, Deceived or Discipled?* (sub-titled *The Search for Truth in a Multicultural Society*). This covers many subject areas in lots of short chapters and includes the chapter *Sexuality and Faith*. Dr Panter answers many basic questions in a straightforward, honest and simple way, from a medical perspective but always informed by his Christian faith (ISBN 978-974-16-5197-9, published by actsco.org in Thailand).

It is noteworthy that in the UK (and this is likely to be mirrored elsewhere, but not perhaps to such an extreme) we have an education system that insists on its programme of "sex education". Whilst an understanding of biological realities must always be helpful and valuable, there is no doubt that much so-called sex education is little more than sex propaganda. The more that the UK invests in sex education, the higher the STD and unwanted pregnancies statistics seem to rise. At the time of writing this book there are plans afoot to deny parents the right to remove their children from such lessons, which may well be delivered by people with a very set, and very partisan, agenda. It is rightly observed that there is a *sex education industry* in the UK within which private non-profit institutions secure government funding to cover the costs of their operations. These institutions sometimes enjoy charitable status, although their almost total State funding makes them, in practice, organs of the State. Is this a case of an education "need" being created by those with a vested interest in meeting that "need", largely at the public's expense? Most subjects studied at school these days involve practical lessons and field trips. Does so-called sex education encourage experimentation? The one strategy most likely to preserve innocence, and protect youngsters from early sexual encounters (abstinence) is the one strategy that is sneered at by the education establishment. The London *Times* newspaper had an ironic slant on this question in one of its cartoons, featured under an article on sex education. The cartoon depicts a teenage lad and his female classmate hand in hand, both in school uniform with the inevitable low slung neck tie, absurdly long trouser belt for the lad and mini skirt for the lass. They are standing at an open front door held ajar by a balding father. The caption: "Hello dad. I decided to bring my biology homework back tonight." A joke for the *Times*, but is it so far from reality? An interesting and useful non-Christian short book challenging the orthodoxy on UK sex education, which identifies the private non-profit institutions closely aligned with the UK Department of Education is Dr E S Williams' *The Outrage of Amoral Sex Education* (published in 2006 by Belmont House Publishing, ISBN 0 9548493 0 2). He argues the point in 76 pages that most parents have absolutely no idea what is being taught, and the amoral nature of the "safe sex" message, which is used as a vehicle for promoting the ideology of the sexual revolution against traditional morality. The so-called "education materials" he cites are very often, as the book's title suggests, simply outrageous. Again at the time of writing this book, the UK Department of Education, led by the nose by the sex education industry, is actively considering categorising sex education material on a movie-like censorship categorisation, simply because parents had begun to wake up to the astonishing range of "materials" now being promoted.

If there is a warning in Scripture for those who design and promote sex education (we note it is never called "relationships education"!) with their own worldly agenda, it was given by Jesus in Mark 9: 42 [repeated in Matthew 18: 6–9 and Luke 17: 1–2] taken here from the New International Version: "**if anyone causes one of these little ones who believe in me to sin, it would be better for him to be thrown into the sea with a large millstone tied around his neck**." Jesus always had the highest regard for the welfare of children. It is innocent children who become polluted with the things of the world, and "evolve" by degrees into sinful adults. Those who cause children to sin carry a heavy burden indeed. One day they will be answerable to the God who punishes evil.

So the world teaches sexual experimentation (yes, its official!) but the Bible teaches an approach to building lives and relationships of the utmost fidelity. Jesus affirmed that marriage is good and worthwhile, and He affirmed God's purpose for it, as we explored in Chapter 1. Nowhere in the Bible is it claimed that marriage is easy, that it will be a bed of roses, or that the two having been joined as one will inevitably live happily ever after. But the genius of marriage is that it provides a wonderful medium for love to grow. As suggested earlier in this book, love is not so much the basis for marriage, but rather marriage is the basis for love. It is only within total commitment that the two can truly give themselves to each other. We observed earlier in this book that the existence of a prenuptial agreement, setting out terms to be observed in a divorce, really undermines the marriage at the most foundational level. It means that the element of cleaving is only conditional. Indeed we could go a little further from the *one flesh* perspective in observing this: in this whole God-ordained programme of leaving and cleaving (Genesis 2: 24), where a prenuptial agreement exists, we can say that the couple *did* leave, but *did not* (truly) cleave. Where a cohabitation occurs we can say that the couple *did* cleave, but *did not* truly leave, in the sense we explored in Chapter 1.

Marriage is to be nurtured like a delicate plant in the garden. It will need tender, loving care. The spouses will have to work at it to 'keep the show on the road'. Where the blessing of children is experienced, marriage provides those children with the oxygen of certainty within which they can grow and develop, knowing that tomorrow will be as today, in terms of mum and dad. This is of course why a divorce is so devastating for a child, no matter how you look at it. Animals don't get married – generally speaking they stay together only for a season if at all. The genius of marriage is that it follows a design – God's design – and when it works well, delivers real benefits to those who are married: health benefits, status benefits, even economic benefits. It is to be hoped that none of this sounds smug or superior. All people of goodwill and sensitivity feel for those who have suffered relationship breakdown, no less than marital breakdown. But when it "works", marriage surely provides the best possible design for building lives and relationships.

What it means to be a Christian

Plainly in this book we have been looking at the One Flesh dynamic that God ordained from the earliest time. In chapter 2 we posed five questions that most people must answer at some point:

How should I pick my lifetime's partner?
How should our relationship be founded?
What will be our mutual objectives as we consider the prospect of becoming *one flesh*?
How far should we go in our physical relationship?

In the seven chapters that make up this book we should at the very least have provided a framework within which to consider these matters. We noted that some readers will have had serious questions about God and about the Bible as we travelled this path of exploration together, and they were invited to "park" their questions temporarily. Now is the time they will have to pick them up again. This book cannot possibly have answered all those questions and it was not intended to do so. But readers should have gained a very clear sense of what Jesus taught, what the Bible says and what is God's overarching purpose in marriage. In some respects we would have to agree with the assertion that to keep to the high standards demanded by God is humanly speaking virtually impossible (not impossible, but virtually impossible). But, it has to be said, where we are weak, God is strong. We can receive power from Him, to give us the strength and wisdom we need to live life according to His commands.

We said in chapter 1 that whatever reason we have for choosing to follow Jesus, it should *not* be simply to find a mate! But we should also confirm that it is the testimony of many that, having become Christians, they have found the strength necessary to live out a thoroughly Christian life – and this life is not boring, it is a wonderful, exciting and satisfying journey of discovery! And for very many that journey has also involved finding a o*ne flesh* mate. Asking for God's strength, very many find that the high fidelity demands that God makes on us are able to be met in His power. This is not fanciful. This is reality, just go to your local church and quietly ask some long-married couples! Christian marriage is not easy because Christians who are married face just the same types of temptations, difficulties and pressures that are common to everyone else. And it is probably also fair to say that Christian marriages are *not* easier than the marriages of non-Christians. But it is surely true to say that Christians can appropriate that "X-factor" that makes a real and lasting difference: power from God to live for Him.

So, having provided the tools to go some long way

to answer the five questions above, there is surely one more question in the minds of some readers: ***Just what does it mean to be a Christian and is it something that I could become***? The first part of answering that question will surprise some: must I become a Protestant, a Catholic, a Greek Orthodox? In other words, *which church saves*? The message of Christianity is not to ask Romans or Greeks (for example) to become Protestants. Protestantism has no more power to save than Greek Orthodoxy or Catholicism, in fact. No church can 'save' you, but the risen, living Lord Jesus can. So what did Jesus say? At the beginning of this book we suggested that if people are so unconcerned about their relationships that they cannot be bothered to see what Jesus taught, then they should put down this book and go their own way. Perhaps we must reluctantly make the same comment now. If people are so unconcerned about their relationship with God that they cannot be bothered to see what Jesus said, then maybe now is the time to take up their doubts once again. These doubts may be a convenient "peg" on which to hang the "coat" of unbelief! But for those who do care, now is the right time to explore what Jesus said.

Once again, rather than pasting in text from the Bible to answer this, the reader is encouraged to make his or her own, private study of what Jesus said, and what the apostles taught. To do this you will need a decent translation of the Bible. The author favours the New International Version or the New King James Version, but there are a good number of helpful translations available in modern language. The author would certainly not rule out use of the older Revised Standard Version or the old King James Version (also called the "Authorised Version"), but these do use very old-fashioned language and for some that may be a barrier to seeing clearly what God is saying (although the Holy Spirit will help you to understand even these older versions – it really depends on the reader's attitude and desire).

We all alike are sinners against God
See Psalm 53: 2–3; see Romans 3: 23–24

We cannot save ourselves. We need to be saved from the effects and consequences of our sins. We need to change.
See Romans 4: 22–24

God promised from the earliest time to send a Saviour into the World
See Isaiah 42: 1 – 7; Matthew 1: 20–21

God loved His world as He gave His only Son for you
See John 3: 16–17

Jesus said that it is necessary to be born again
See John 3: 1–21. See 1 Peter 1: 23

These are not 'proof texts' to settle the argument. But they should give readers a sense of what God is saying through Jesus His Son and throughout the witness of Scripture. If you are serious about relationship with God then now is the right time to do some genuine searching. You may well have a Christian friend who can help you. You may have a church near where you live that can help you. But to get any further you have to begin to see your need, your own rebelliousness against God. He loves you.

He sent His Son for You. He sent His Son to stand in your place and receive the punishment that actually should have been awarded to you. But the final decision is in your hands. Will you repent toward God (not just feeling sorry, but turn away from sin) and *believe in* Jesus? That "believing" includes *trusting* Him and starting to be His *disciple*, learning from Him, seeking to be immersed in and filled with His Holy Spirit. Following Him involves obeying Him, and includes your response the call to be baptised. The wonderful dimensions of new life in Christ known and experienced by believers are simply and clearly explained in a new (2012) book entitled *The Seven Wonders of His Story* by David Pawson (Anchor Recordings Ltd).

Many will already have a sense that there is something missing in their lives and would like to find out once and for all what that something is. Here is an interesting thought: your name, whether you are a male or a female, is Peter. I repeat, *you are Peter*, and there's absolutely no getting away from it! But that requires some explanation so let's dig a little more into it! There is one question that absolutely everyone in this world has to answer, sooner or later. Whilst we may ignore the question and so refuse to answer it directly, even in ignoring it we are making our answer, albeit a negative one! In the New Testament some time shortly after the miracle that we call 'the feeding of the five thousand', Jesus asked a question about what today we might call His public image. We pick up the story in Luke 9: 18 [but it is repeated in Matthew 16: 13–19 and Mark 8: 27–29].

One day when Jesus was praying alone, the disciples came to him. "Who do the crowds say I am?" he asked them.

"Some say that you are John the Baptist," they answered. "Others say that you are Elijah, while others say that one of the prophets of long ago has come back to life."

"What about you?" he asked them. "Who do you say I am?"

Peter answered, "You are God's Messiah."

Luke 9: 18–20

This was the "Peter question". It was no idle question. Jesus was teaching His disciples what they needed to confront – His *identity*. They all knew that God was going to send a Messiah (or "Christ" to use the English from the Greek translation of the word). In first-century Judea the coming of God's *Messiah* or *Saviour* was anticipated with a sense of urgency. The question was at the back of everyone's mind. Could Jesus be the Messiah? "What about you? Who do you say that I am?" We get a sense of the disciples' reluctance to respond. Who would have the courage to say that Jesus was God's long awaited anointed one – the Messiah? Probably you could have heard a pin drop once Jesus asked the question. There would have been a pause as the disciples looked at each other. It was an electrifying moment. It was bold and often headstrong Peter who broke the silence. Although he could not really understand the full implications of what he was saying, Peter got the answer right. And now we turn to you, dear reader. Your (other) name is "Peter". There is no getting away from it! And like Peter in the Bible, it is *you* who have to answer this question! Who do you say that Jesus is? Your relationship with Him through eternity will be settled by your answer. It is a serious question that requires a serious answer.

Back in chapter 5 we were introduced to the idea of the Kinsman Redeemer. It was Boaz, who was a relative of Naomi, and through Naomi a relative of Ruth. It was the "life" of Naomi and Ruth that Boaz redeemed, by buying their land and providing a future for them in the shape of offspring to the lovely Ruth whom Boaz dutifully and joyfully married. To meet the Ruth's needs, a suitor had to be a kinsman. To meet our needs, Jesus is our "Kinsman" – that is why God sent His Son in the flesh (as a human) to live for us, and to die for us. Only a man could achieve what Jesus did. It was only a man who could satisfy the needs of justice. Jesus is a Man, "Son of Man", and He has stepped up to the mark. He has lived for me (and you). And He has died for me (and you). And, we might add, He has been raised once more to life for me (and for you).

It is hoped that this book has lived up to its subtitle, being a study of "What Jesus teaches about love, relationships, marriage and a lot more...." There is a wedding to which you are invited, dear reader. And no, it is not your own wedding, although that may one day be your joy if it has not been already. At the end of each chapter in this book, readers will have seen the line "Happy are those who have been invited to the wedding feast". But the phrase was deliberately truncated. It is not the full line. It comes from Revelation chapter 19 in the Bible, and specifically from verse 9, *"Happy are those who have been invited to the wedding feast of the Lamb."* The Lamb is Jesus and He is returning one day (perhaps soon) for His people. Jesus is the Lamb that was slain from the beginning of the world. Readers will remember that it was in the Garden of Eden, at the beginning of the world, that mankind rebelled, in the shape of Adam and Eve who wanted to be "like God", knowing right from wrong. The crucifixion happened once, in history, but that sacrificial death was needed from the moment of mankind's rebellion.

Jesus is the sacrificial Lamb, given for me (and for you). Since He has accepted the punishment that should have come to me (and you), what are we to do? A response is required – of repentance and faith on the one hand – or of rejection on the other. The choice is that stark. I can only say that, having made the choice – some thirty-plus years ago – to repent toward God and believe in and follow Jesus, I have no regrets, and rejoice each day at the journey of faith with Jesus. I know the one Who has paid my price, and I know that I shall be with Him forever, so long as I go on being His disciple. The invitation is RSVP – it does require a response!

We want to build our relationships in such a way that they are beneficial, happy and successful. God has set out a plan, a directive, an ordinance, that in male-female relationships the couple shall leave and cleave and become one flesh. Within this sort of relationship there are challenges and difficulties, to be sure, but there are also exquisite joys. It was God's good plan, and we would expect it to be the best plan. Hopefully in these pages readers will have got a sense of how to build relationships that honour God, that honour you, and that honour your intended, whom you may not even have met, as you read these lines! Is not he or she worth honouring now? If you have not yet had your wedding, should you be called towards a married life, then I hope your special day yields all you want it to. But there is another wedding to which you are invited. RSVP!

"Happy are those who have been invited to the wedding feast of the Lamb"

Kingdom Seekers Mike Endicott

What does it mean to seek first the Kingdom of God? Mike Endicott (author of *Heaven's Dynamite*, *Christian Healing*, *Rediscovering Kingdom Healing* and *Pilgrimage*) encourages us to become kingdom seekers. He sets out exciting truths about God's kingdom, showing us something of its attractiveness as well as its centrality to all genuine Christian life and witness. Jesus affirmed that He is the way, the truth and the life, and the author explores some of the powerful implications of that revelation.

The Bible Student Ed. Peter Sammons

50 exciting studies to help us to explore what the Bible says today!
* Does God speak today through the pages of the Bible?
* What is God's message on the key questions that life throws up?
* How consistent is God's revelation in the Old and New Testaments?
 An accessible resource for personal and group study, with helpful insights and discussion points for preachers, teachers and all who want to examine key questions in the twenty-first century. Inspired by Joe Church's *Every Man a Bible Student*, this is a completely revised and updated book, containing new studies and entirely reformatted. Five authors contributed studies: Rev Alex Jacob, Rev David M Moore, Greg Stevenson, Rev Peter Byron-Davies, Peter Sammons.

Ready or Not – He is Coming Stephanie Cottam

The Bible speaks of Jesus as the Bridegroom, and His followers as His Bride. The Day of His return for her will be a glorious day of rejoicing – but what exactly does all of this mean? What can we learn from the traditional Jewish wedding customs about "that glorious Day"? What does the relationship between a Jewish Bride and her groom tell us of our relationship with our Saviour, Jesus? And what does it mean for the Bride to have "prepared herself"? In *Ready or Not – He is Coming* Stephanie Cottam explores the biblical marriage rites in the light of Christian revelation and brings Jesus' simile to life in a straightforward and disarmingly simple way, but with a stark warning: Jesus was crystal clear that when He returns, not everyone will be ready for Him. Some will make their excuses and decline His invitation. Some of His watchmen will be asleep, spiritually speaking. A high proportion of foolish maidens will have no oil in their lamps – both groups will be left outside the wedding feast. What sort of a follower of Jesus are you? Are you prepared and ready – or half asleep, seeking other diversions during His long absence?

ONGOING STUDY – FURTHER MATERIALS

MULTIMEDIA

Recovering a Biblical Perspective of Sexuality
Rev John Atkinson
2 x DVD set of 5 talks + associated PDF study materials
on same disks (2006).
Google the title and author name for distributors.

BOOKS

Deluded, Deceived or Discipled?
The Search for Truth in a Multicultural Society
(Especially Chapter 12)
Dr Martin Panter
ISBN 978-974-16-5197-9 (August 2008)
Publisher: actsco.org

Let Love Be Your Greatest
A series of 12 short studies originally published as a
correspondence course
Delores Friesen
Publisher: Editions Trobisch, Germany, 1978
(published in English)

Marriage and The Family
Dr A J Higgins
ISBN 0-948417-29-3 (1988) (Republished and up-dated
twice since and available commercially at time of writing)
Publisher: Gospel Tract Publications

Mere Christianity
(Especially chapters 5 and 6 of Section 3 of the book)
C S Lewis
Various Publishers and ISBNs
– available commercially at time of writing

Church and State in the New Millennium
– Issues of Belief and Morality for the 21st Century
(various chapters, various subjects)
Rev David Holloway
ISBN 0 00 274060 5 Publisher: Harper Collins (2000)